BOOST
YOUR BRAIN

BOOST
YOUR BRAIN

JOEL LEVY

DK

LONDON, NEW YORK, MELBOURNE,
MUNICH, AND DELHI

Illustrator Keith Hagan
Project Editor Elizabeth Yeates
US Senior Editor Shannon Beatty
US Editor Jill Hamilton
Senior Designer Miranda Harvey
Editor Angela Baynham
Designer Harriet Yeomans
Senior Pre-Producer Tony Phipps
Senior Producer Jen Scothern
Creative Technical Support Sonia Charbonnier
Managing Editor Dawn Henderson
Managing Art Editor Christine Keilty
Art Director Peter Luff
Publisher Peggy Vance

First American edition, 2014

Published in the United States by
DK Publishing, 375 Hudson Street,
New York, NY 10014

14 15 16 17 18 10 9 8 7 6 5 4 3 2 1
001–192146–Jan/2014

Copyright © 2014 Dorling Kindersley Limited

A CIP catalog record for this book is available
from the Library of Congress.
ISBN 978-1-4654-0847-1

DK books are available at special discounts for
bulk purchases for sales promotions, premiums,
fund-raising, or educational use. For details,
contact: DK Publishing Special Markets,
375 Hudson Street, New York, NY 10014
or SpecialSales@dk.com

Printed and bound by South China
Printing Co., China

**Discover more at
www.dk.com**

Contents

Introduction

Everyday life can push your mental abilities to the limit, whether it's remembering yet another website password or recalling the names of the people you were briefly introduced to at a dinner party. This book offers an intensive program to help you face such challenges head on, with exercises and puzzles designed to boost all areas of your mental performance. In addition, it provides techniques and tips to tackle cognitive conundrums, giving you the expertise and confidence you need to overcome life's intellectual obstacles.

Before beginning your mental workout, take a moment to look at how your brain works and get acquainted with some helpful jargon. In everyday life you call on a variety of mental skills, which can be divided into two main types: memory and cognition. Memory covers everything from comparing prices in your head when shopping to recalling facts you learned at school. Cognition is a technical term for thinking, and includes intelligence, problem solving, creativity, and language aptitude.

MEMORY

Nobody really knows for sure precisely how memory works, but experiments have suggested a model that seems like an accurate description: the multistore model. According to this there are different stages of memory. Information detected by your senses floods into your brain and is held for only a second in a sensory register. Automatic filtering processes then let some of this information through into your short-term memory, which is sometimes known as working memory.

Only a few items of information can be held at a time in your short-term memory, and remain for approximately 30 seconds before being either lost rapidly to decay and/or interference, or refreshed and reinforced through attention and repetition. For example, when you need to remember a phone number long enough to dial it, it's short-term memory that you are using—it is unlikely that you would remember the number for a long period of time. If, however, the material is interesting, emotional, chimes with other memories already stored, or if you make a conscious effort to rehearse and learn it, the material can be laid down as long-term memory, where an unlimited amount of information can remain indefinitely. Knowing how to tie your shoelaces is an example of long-term memory—it is continually "stored" in your memory.

The laying down of material, and a memory, is called encoding. For information to be encoded and stored into your long-term memory, it must first pass through short-term memory. When encoded, memories are stored until you need to access them through the process known as recall. Encoding and recall are the two sides of the memory coin—unless you are able to do both of them, you won't remember something.

It is worth identifying an intermediate category, medium-term memory, which covers the area where short-term shades into long-term memory. Here, material can remain for approximately a week; it is the information that is not processed immediately from short-term to long-term memory, but will eventually either be stored in your long-term memory (through encoding) or will decay and be lost.

Long-term memory itself comes in several varieties. For instance, knowledge of skills, from driving a car to

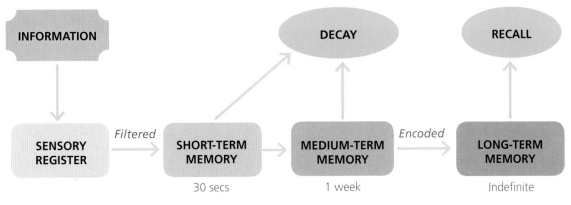

Multistore memory model

typing to tying your shoelaces, is called procedural memory—the "how" rather than "what." Memory for "what," such as "what year did the First World War begin?" is called declarative or explicit memory, and this itself breaks down into several forms. Episodic memory, for instance, is your memory for episodes and events in your life—events that have happened to you—and this includes a particular subset of episodic memory known as biographical memory. Biographical memory holds all your memorable personal experiences and is one of the most important forms of memory, as it is crucial to our sense of self.

Many problems and frustrations in everyday life are linked to poor or underperforming memory— from struggling to get into your online accounts to forgetting the one shopping item you went out for. Practicing ways to improve each stage of memory formation and retrieval can improve mental performance in the short and long term; it may even help to counteract age-related memory decline.

COGNITION

If memories are like the ingredients you store in your mental "larder," cognition is your ability to cook with them. Just as you might be good at chopping vegetables or an expert at baking, but hopeless at carving a roast or seasoning a sauce, the same applies to your mental processing, which breaks down into several subtypes or aptitudes. You may be more proficient in one area of cognition, and may need a little more practice in another.

Verbal, or linguistic, aptitude is your ability with words and language, which enables you to complete crossword puzzles and determines whether you can turn a phrase or spell a tricky word. Numerical aptitude is probably the area that elicits the most negative reactions, thanks to what is known as math phobia.

Visuo-spatial aptitude covers your ability to think about shape, form, and space, and to represent physical space in your mind's eye. It determines how good you are at reading maps and finding your way, or holding a shape in your mind and then moving it around.

Logical aptitude is your ability to think rationally and solve puzzles, whether they involve words, numbers, or symbols. It underlies your ability to crack codes and solve puzzles such as Sudoku. Finally, creativity is an aspect of intelligence that covers your ability to make new and unexpected connections between ideas and be original and flexible in your thinking.

This is not the complete picture of intelligence; there is a whole other side to intelligence called emotional or social intelligence, which concerns your ability to recognize, control, and deal with your emotions and those of others. However, emotional intelligence is much more subjective and personal than rational intelligence, and doesn't lend itself to exercises and puzzles.

JUMP TO IT

So, that's enough theory. Take a look at the pages on "How to use this book," then start at Chapter 1 (or the chapter most relevant to you) and enjoy boosting your brain!

How to use this book

Boost Your Brain specifically addresses the mental challenges of modern living, with short, easily digested chapters that focus on a specific area, such as improving memory for passwords and PINs or tackling short-term forgetfulness—"where did I put my keys?" Complete the exercises and learn memory-enhancing and brain-boosting techniques to give your brain a complete mental workout. Then discover how well you've performed and how you can improve.

WORKING THROUGH THE BOOK

The book is divided into 13 chapters, each focusing on areas concerned with mental-agility challenges that can occur in everyday life, such as PINs, passwords, appointments, directions, and many more. You can go straight to the chapter and area you feel you need to work on most, or proceed through the book systematically for an all-round mental fitness program.

The first seven chapters focus on memory; Chapters 1–3 on short-term memory, Chapter 4 on medium-term memory, and Chapters 5–7 on long-term memory. Each of these chapters is task-orientated to maximize practical impact. For instance, Chapter 2 focuses on the problem of forgetting new names and faces, Chapter 6 targets the problem posed by the plethora of passwords and PINs people need to remember, and Chapter 7 explains techniques that can help improve your revision.

The remaining chapters deal with specific sub-types of intelligence. Chapters 8 and 9 deal with numerical intelligence, Chapter 10 with verbal intelligence, and Chapter 11 with visuo-spatial intelligence. Chapter 12 deals with logical reasoning, including riddles and codebreaking, while Chapter 13 focuses on creativity and lateral thinking.

Each chapter begins with a quick quiz to allow you to assess your capability in that particular field. You then dive straight into the exercises, puzzles, tips, and techniques.

Apart from Chapter 13, each chapter has a scoring system, which allows you to assess whether your brain is the best it can be or whether you need more practice. For Chapter 13, assess your own creativity by referring back to the exercises. Did you feel challenged by the activity? What would you do differently with hindsight?

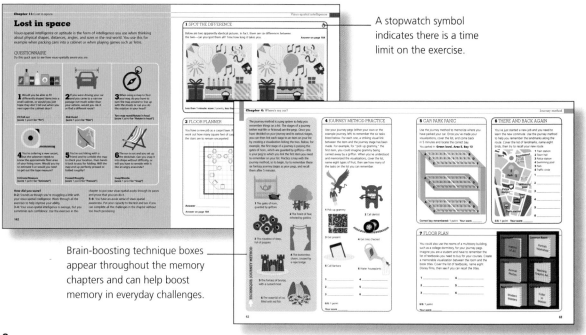

A stopwatch symbol indicates there is a time limit on the exercise.

Brain-boosting technique boxes appear throughout the memory chapters and can help boost memory in everyday challenges.

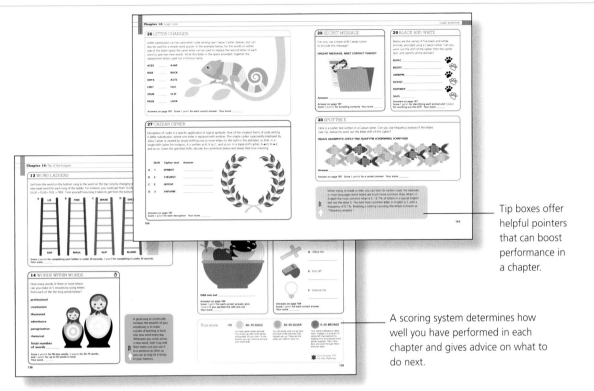

Tip boxes offer helpful pointers that can boost performance in a chapter.

A scoring system determines how well you have performed in each chapter and gives advice on what to do next.

TECHNIQUES AND TIPS

In the memory chapters, you will find in-depth explanations of memory-enhancing techniques and devices, known as mnemonics. These are strategies that top memory experts use to perform amazing feats of recall. These may seem challenging at first, but keep practising and they will become second nature, providing you with a powerful memory tool that you can use in many different aspects of daily life. Each chapter also has a tip box, offering quick tips to boost performance.

TIMED TASKS AND BREAKS

Many of the exercises are time-limited to mimic "real-life" conditions, and these are indicated by a stopwatch symbol. In addition, many of the memory exercises suggest "time-lag" tasks, such as thinking of eight types of flower, for you to do between committing something to memory (encoding) and testing for recall. These time lags prevent you from mentally rehearsing the test material between encoding and recall by forcing you to focus on something else. You don't have to do the time lag task if you don't want to; you can just wait for a few minutes or create your own time lag, by making a cup of tea for example.

SOLUTIONS

You will find the answers to the exercises for Chapters 1 to 12 at the back of the book (there's no scoring in Chapter 13). Add up your points and check the scoring system at the end of each chapter to see how well you performed. If you answered some of the exercises incorrectly, can you see where you went wrong? Look at the techniques and tips for guidance and try the exercises again. Even if you answered the exercises correctly, there is always room for improvement. See if you can challenge yourself further by solving the puzzles more quickly, or using the tips and techniques in your everyday life.

CHALLENGES

Each chapter continues with a Challenge, which can be found at the back of the book. The Challenges are tasks to carry out at home, or during your daily routine. They are designed to lend a helping hand if your score in a chapter was disappointing, so that you can try to improve further in that area. Even if you scored well in a particular chapter, the Challenges are worth trying, as they can help to hone and maintain your mental abilities. The best way to keep your mind in tiptop condition is to keep using it, so keep referring to the Challenges to boost your brain beyond this book.

CHAPTER 1
QUICK FIX
SHORT-TERM MEMORY

Quick fix

Short-term memory (STM) is the human equivalent of RAM (random access memory) in a computer in that it is easy to manipulate and process, but also easy to erase and quick to fade. Is your short-term memory functional or failing?

QUESTIONNAIRE
Use this quick quiz to get an instant rating of your STM skills.

1 Do you ever walk into a room and then realize you've forgotten why you went into it?

Yes/No [score 1 point for "No"]

2 When replying to questions by email, do you have to keep scrolling down the original email to see what the questions are?

Yes/No [score 1 point for "No"]

3 You're on the phone and someone tells you a phone number; do you need to write it down right away, or can you wait until the phone call is over?

Write/Wait [score 1 point for "Wait"]

4 You have called a taxi to come and pick you up from the airport. Can you remember the license plate the firm gives you, so you can spot your waiting taxi among all the cars?

Yes/No [score 1 point for "Yes"]

5 Stopping to ask for directions, you receive a list of six instructions. Will you have to stop and ask again before you reach your destination?

Yes/No [score 1 point for "No"]

6 At the bar with six friends you take the drink orders. Do you need to write them down, or can you remember all of them without help?

Write/Remember [score 1 point for "Remember"]

How did you score?

0–2: Your STM needs urgent attention. Give it a workout with the exercises in this chapter and check out the Challenge on page 178 for further development.

3–4: Your STM is average. Work on boosting it with this chapter's tests and quizzes.

5–6: Your STM is awesome! See if you can score top marks in the exercises that follow.

1 RANDOM OBJECT RECALL

Identify each of these objects and spell out the name of the object backward. When you've done all eight, cover up the images and, using your STM, see if you can write down the whole list.

1 _____

2 _____

3 _____

4 _____

5 _____

6 _____

7 _____

8 _____

8/8: 1 point

Your score _____

2 WHERE DID YOU GET THAT HAT?

Can you spot the odd one out in this collection of hats? Once you've spotted it, cover up the pictures, then write down all the different types of hats your STM can recall.

1 _____

2 _____

3 _____

4 _____

5 _____

6 _____

6/6: 1 point

Your score _____

Answer on page 180

13

3 THESE CARDS WILL SELF-DESTRUCT

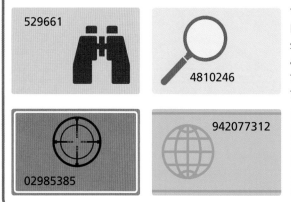

529661

4810246

942077312

02985385

3826564902

You're at a conference for spies, and some delegates have given you their business cards with their unique spy codes. There's just one hitch: the cards self-destruct after 30 seconds. Can you remember the numbers on the cards? For each number, read it once, cover it up then write it down on a piece of paper.

What was the longest number you got right?
10 digits: 5 points
9 digits: 4 points
8 digits: 3 points
7 digits: 2 points
6 digits: 1 point
Your score _____

4 ZOO TIME

Below are nine very different types of animals. Look at them for 30 seconds, then cover them up and see if you can recall all nine.

1 _____
2 _____
3 _____
4 _____
5 _____
6 _____
7 _____
8 _____
9 _____

9/9: 3 points
8/9: 2 points
7/9: 1 point

Your score _____

5 BIRD TIME

Below are nine quite similar animals. Look at them for 30 seconds, then cover them up and see how your STM fares when you try to list all nine.

1 _____
2 _____
3 _____
4 _____
5 _____
6 _____
7 _____
8 _____
9 _____

9/9: 3 points
8/9: 2 points
7/9: 1 point

Your score _____

6 CAN YOU CUT IT?

Circle the items below that you would be able to cut with a knife.

Answer on page 180

Now cover the pictures and answer the questions below. Even though you weren't trying to memorize the objects, your STM has probably stored some of the details about them.

**What is on
top of the cupcake?** _____

**What is the logo on the
side of the teakettle?** _____

**What color is
the iron cord?** _____

How many scoops of ice cream are there?
_____

Score **1 point** for each correct answer

Your score _____

7 AT THE SUPERMARKET

This exercise is another example of how your STM records information, such as locating and grouping, without you realizing. Which of these foods do you prefer to eat cooked, and which raw? Mark a "C" or an "R" above each item then cover the pictures.

SHELF

DELI COUNTER

CAN DISPLAY

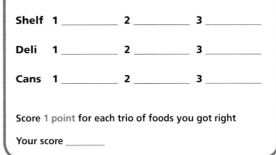

Can you remember which foods were where?

Shelf 1 _____ 2 _____ 3 _____

Deli 1 _____ 2 _____ 3 _____

Cans 1 _____ 2 _____ 3 _____

Score **1 point** for each trio of foods you got right

Your score _____

8 BAR SIGNS

Here are eight bar signs. Study them for 5 seconds each, then cover them all and fill in the missing colors on the signs next door, writing the name of each bar below.

8 names and colours/8: 5 points 7/8: 4 points
6/8: 3 points 5/8: 2 points 4/8: 1 point

Your score _____

The Drunken Dog

Twisty McPhee's

The Roadside Inn

The Sports Bar

Maltese Cross

The Iron Horse

Whistler's Mother

The Fruit Lounge

9 TRAFFIC SIGNS

Traffic police are launching a crackdown on inattentive drivers who ignore the signs they see. Look through each sequence of signs separately for 10 seconds, cover it up, and fill in the blank below the sequence.

Score 1 point for each correct answer

Your score _____

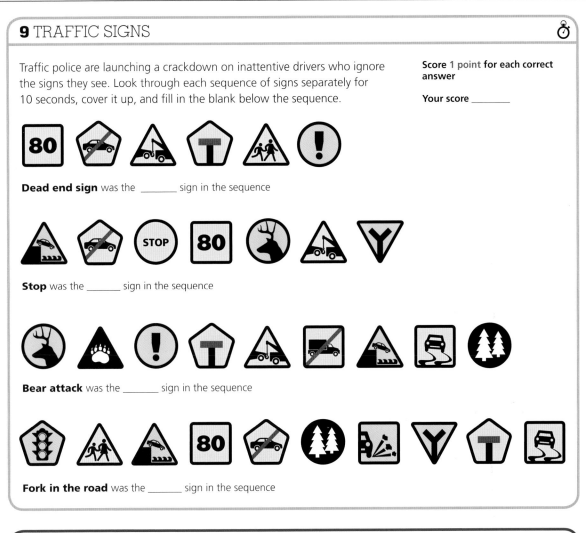

Dead end sign was the _____ sign in the sequence

Stop was the _____ sign in the sequence

Bear attack was the _____ sign in the sequence

Fork in the road was the _____ sign in the sequence

10 DRAWING WITH YOUR MIND'S EYE

Can you draw a picture in your mind's eye and remember it for long enough to put it down on paper? Follow the instructions below in your head, cover the instructions, and draw what you can see in your mind's eye in the space provided.

Imagine a circle.
A square fits exactly inside the circle, touching the sides.
A diagonal line divides the square in half, running from top left to bottom right.
Sitting on top of the circle is a small triangle.
In the bottom left corner of the square is a black spot.

Score 2 points if your picture looks like the answer on page 180

Your score _____

11 DUCKS IN A ROW

You are stuck in a traffic jam caused by a line of seven unusual ducks crossing the road. Look at the seven ducks in the top row, and then cover them up and look at the seven ducks in the bottom row. Draw a circle around any duck that was *not* crossing the road.

Answer on page 180   **Score 1 point for each different duck you spotted   Your score** _____

12 TRAIL BLAZER

You are leading a hike across dangerous country, but you only manage to glance at your map before a gust of wind blows it away. Look at the map on the left for 30 seconds, and then cover it up and fill in the appropriate landmarks on the blank map on the right.

Score 1 point for remembering all the landmarks   Your score _____

13 CHILD'S PLAY

Your toddler has been playing with the jewelry from a drawer in your jewelry box and has left five items on your bedside table. The first picture below shows how the drawer looked before she started playing with its contents. Look at this picture for 30 seconds, cover it up, and then draw arrows linking the items below the second picture to their rightful spots in the jewelry box.

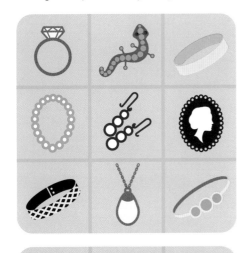

Score 1 point for each piece of jewelry you put back in the right place

Your score _____

14 TREASURE ISLAND

A drunken pirate hands you a map of an island and gives you directions for finding treasure, before he passes out. Read once through the directions below and then cover them up.
Then trace a path across the map, following the directions, starting from the spot marked "X."

Directions:
A Go north until you reach the third palm tree and then head west.
B Cross the swamp and the river to reach the cave.
C Head north across the mountains to the beach.
D Turn east and follow the river upstream to the third waterfall.

Where did you end up? _____

Answer on page 180
Score 1 point for landing at the correct place

Your score _____

19

15 RACING COLORS

There's panic at the Grand Prix as unusual weather conditions have resulted in mud all over the paintwork on the racing cars. Can you help restore their racing liveries by reading through the team color descriptions in the program (right), covering the descriptions, and then coloring in the cars below, one team at a time? If you don't have colored pens or pencils handy, just write in the name of the color.

Team Boost: Green front fender, blue nose, red cockpit, orange body, yellow rear fender
Team Sprint: Blue front fender, orange nose, yellow cockpit, blue body, green rear fender
Team SuperX: Red front fender, orange nose, green cockpit, yellow body, blue rear fender

Team WarpSpeed: Blue front fender, red nose, orange cockpit, green body, yellow rear fender
Team Vanish: Yellow front fender, orange nose, red cockpit, blue body, green rear fender

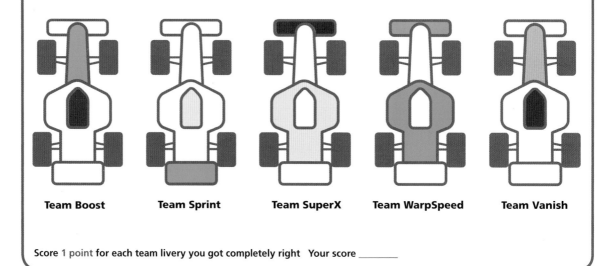

| Team Boost | Team Sprint | Team SuperX | Team WarpSpeed | Team Vanish |

Score 1 point for each team livery you got completely right   **Your score** _____

16 CONTEXT IS KING

 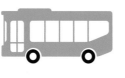

A At a tennis match: the order of priorities for survival is shelter, water, food.

B On a bus: the scientific notation for the element gold is Au.

C In the rain: the capital of Uruguay is Montevideo.

The trouble with STM is that things can slip out of it as quickly as they go in. One way to fix things more firmly in your STM is to pay close attention to the context in which you receive information. Try this out by reading the three facts on the left in the context of the suggested scenario. You'll be tested on the information later in the chapter.

17 CHESS CHALLENGE

You are playing chess in the park, but the wind keeps blowing over the pieces. For each game below, look at the first board for 30 seconds, then cover it up and reproduce it on the empty board alongside.

Score 2 points for each board you got right

Your score _____

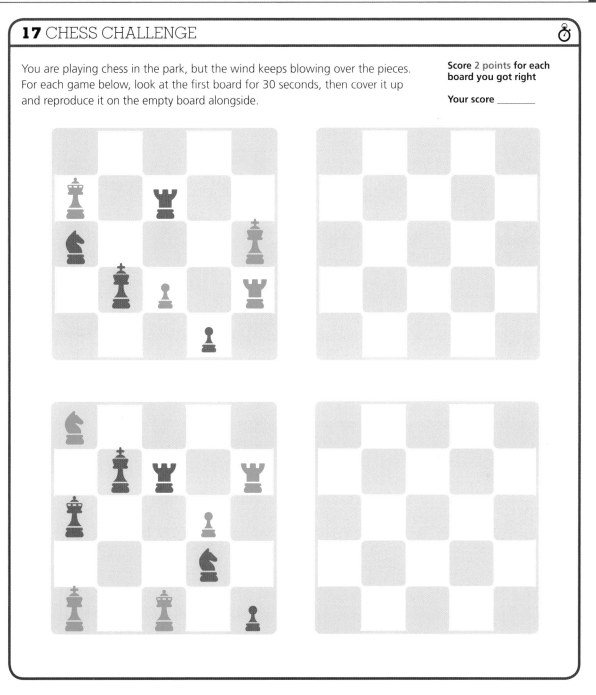

18 KIM'S GAME

In Rudyard Kipling's 1901 novel *Kim,* part of a spy's education involves memory training. In this simple game, memorize the objects below for 30 seconds and then cover them up. On a separate piece of paper, list as many objects as you can.

14–15: 3 points
12–13: 2 points
10–11: 1 point

Your score _____

TECHNIQUE: CHUNKING

Chunking means organizing information into chunks. Your STM can handle only around seven pieces of information at a time, but if you can organize multiple bits into a single chunk, it may help you cram more in. Try memorizing these 14 objects as seven pairs. Then cover them up, wait 30 seconds, and on a separate piece of paper, see if you can list them all.

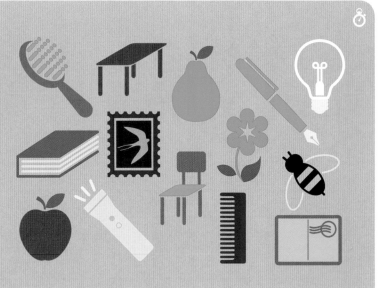

19 KIM'S GAME: HARD

The objects below are more similar to each other than those in exercise 18 and therefore less memorable. Using chunking, pair up the items and see how many you can recall when you cover them up after 30 seconds of memorizing.

14: 5 points **12–13:** 4 points
10–11: 3 points **7–9:** 2 points
6: 1 point

Your score _____

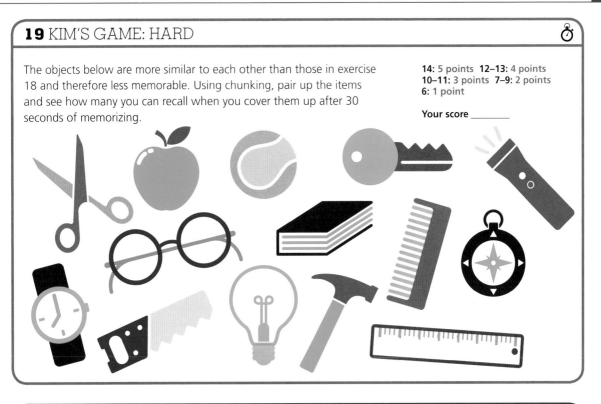

20 KIM'S GAME: FIENDISH

Only memory champions will succeed in this tough challenge! Using chunking, give yourself 30 seconds to memorize these 30 items, then see how many of them you can write down on a piece of paper.

25–30: 10 points **17–24:** 8 points
12–16: 6 points **10–11:** 4 points
8–9: 3 points **6–7:** 2 points **5:** 1 point

Your score _____

21 CONTEXT IS KING

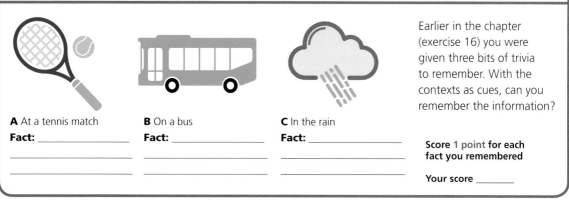

A At a tennis match
Fact: _____
_____
_____

B On a bus
Fact: _____
_____
_____

C In the rain
Fact: _____
_____
_____

Earlier in the chapter (exercise 16) you were given three bits of trivia to remember. With the contexts as cues, can you remember the information?

Score 1 point for each fact you remembered

Your score _____

22 FADE AWAY

STM is especially vulnerable to "decay," where the information stored fades away and is forgotten. People with less decay have better memories. For a quick test of your decay rate, see if you can remember the answers to some of the previous questions:

1. Name two of the types of hat from exercise number 2 "Where did you get that hat?"

_____   _____

2. Which hat was the odd one out in that exercise? _____

Score 1 point for each correct answer

Your score _____

3. Name four of the animals from exercise number 5 "Bird time."

_____   _____

_____   _____

4. From the technique on "Chunking," name one of the object pairs. _____

5. Name two of the objects from exercise 18 "Kim's game."

_____

_____

23 BACKGROUND NOISE

Keeping information in your STM becomes much harder when you are coping with distractions. Try this exercise, for instance: on the right is a hand of cards—can you memorize the hand in 30 seconds while counting backward from 113 in multiples of 3 (i.e. 110, 107, 104, and so on)? When the time is up, cover the cards and write down the hand.

5/5: 2 points 4/5: 1 point   Your score _____

24 INTERFERING OBJECTS

Another problem with STM is called "interference." This is where new information coming in to your STM interferes with previous storage, causing you to forget it. How well can you cope with interference?

A Give yourself 30 seconds to memorize the set of objects below, then cover them up and move on to task B.

7/7: 3 points 5–6/7: 2 points 3–4/7: 1 point

Your score _____

B Draw a circle around the odd one out.

Answer on page 180

C Can you remember the objects memorized in part A?

1 _____   5 _____

2 _____   6 _____

3 _____   7 _____

4 _____

25 INTERFERING NUMBERS

Try another exercise to see how well you can cope with interference.

A Memorize this sequence of numbers for 10 seconds, then cover them up: **4 2 9 0 6 4 8**

B What comes next in this series of playing cards?

_____

Answer on page 180

C What were the numbers you memorized? _____

7/7: 2 points 6/7: 1 point

Your score _____

26 NATURAL WONDERS

Retrieving things from your STM is much easier when you have a cue or trigger to help you remember the information. Allow 30 seconds to remember which natural wonder is in which country, then cover the list.

Angel Falls: Venezuela   **Mount Everest:** Nepal

Table Mountain: South Africa

Great Barrier Reef: Australia

Blue Grotto: Italy

Kilimanjaro: Tanzania

Grand Canyon: USA

Now using the list of countries below, write down the natural wonder associated with each.

Australia:_____

Nepal:_____

Tanzania:_____

Italy:_____

USA:_____

South Africa:_____

Venezuela: _____

Score **1 point** for each correct answer

Your score _____

27 LOVE LINKS

Information with emotional content or associations is often easier to remember. Read through this list of relationships, then cover it all and answer the question.

Ben and Omar are old school friends.

Ted and Katie have been married for 40 years.

Dave is falling in love with Zoe.

John and Orla are having a baby together.

Jessica and Bill are getting divorced.

Karen and Dave are having an affair.

Winona and Desirée are identical twins.

Which couple is having a baby? _____

Score **1 point** for a correct answer

Your score _____

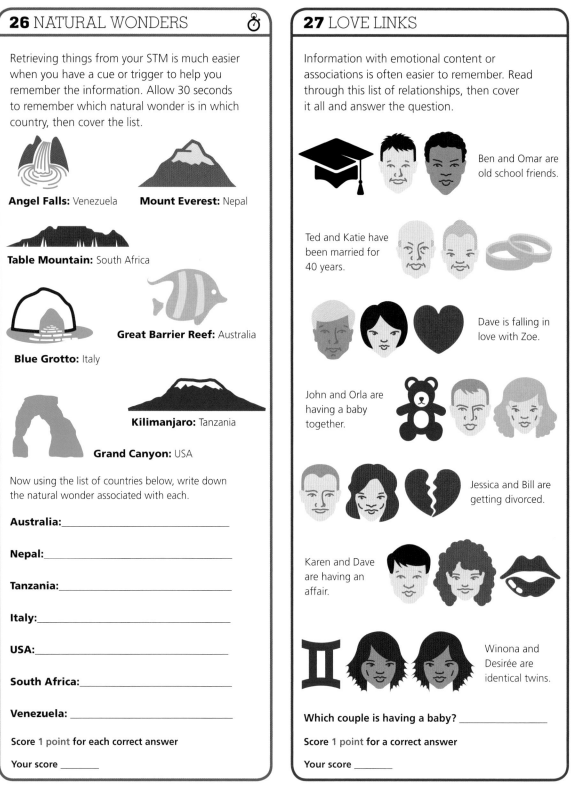

TECHNIQUE: ASSOCIATIONS

Another way to fix new information more firmly in your STM is to build associations between it and information you already know, such as famous names and faces. For instance, try remembering a hand of cards by associating the individual cards with famous names. For example, study the cards below and the associated famous names for 30 seconds. Then cover the cards and spell out the titles of three of your favorite films. Can you remember the cards by thinking of their association?

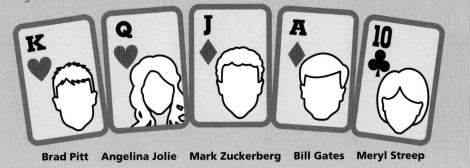

Brad Pitt   Angelina Jolie   Mark Zuckerberg   Bill Gates   Meryl Streep

28 DRINKS ORDER

It's your turn to go to the bar, but you don't have a pen and paper to write down the drinks. To remember the order, associate each drink below with the face or name of the friend who ordered it. Can you remember who ordered which drink?

Charles wants **champagne**

Adam wants a **martini**

Martin wants a **pint of beer**

Brenda wants a **glass of red wine**

Val wants a **pint of stout**

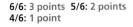

Don wants a **bottle of lager**

6/6: 3 points 5/6: 2 points
4/6: 1 point

Your score _____

Your score   /100   **80–100 GOLD**

Your STM is excellent, but to maintain and maximize high performance it may help to try the Challenge on page 178.

30–79 SILVER

Your STM could be improved. Go back and look at the tips for STM boosting, and check out the Challenge on page 178.

0–29 BRONZE

Your STM needs work. Try the exercises in the chapter again to help boost your performance.

★ Turn to page 178 for the Challenge.

CHAPTER 2

DINNER PARTY GENIUS
NAMES AND FACES

Dinner party genius

Humans have specialized brains and mental processes for perceiving and recognizing faces. Unfortunately, memory often lets us down—especially when we fail to transfer name–face associations from short-term to long-term memory.

QUESTIONNAIRE
Use this quick quiz to get an instant rating of your memory for names and faces.

1 On a long flight you get chatting with the person sitting next to you. Do you have to ask his name more than once?

Likely/Unlikely [score 1 point for "Unlikely"]

2 At a conference you are introduced to a delegate without a name badge. Will you remember her name when speaking to her later in the day?

Yes/No [score 1 point for "Yes"]

At a family birthday party you bump into a distant cousin you haven't seen for 15 years. Can you remember his name?

3 At a family birthday party you bump into a distant cousin you haven't seen for 15 years. Can you remember his name?

Likely/Unlikely [score 1 point for "Likely"]

4 Can you remember the names and describe the features of a colleague's husband and children?

Likely/Unlikely [score 1 point for "Likely"]

5 You arrive at a party and your host introduces you to someone by the door. After mingling for an hour, would you recognize the guest you met at the door?

Likely/Unlikely [score 1 point for "Likely"]

6 Your young daughter tells you about her new friend at school. Next day, your daughter comes out of school with her new pal. Can you remember the friend's name?

Likely/Unlikely [score 1 point for "Likely"]

How did you score?
0–2: Your memory for names and faces needs work, and may prove to be seriously embarrassing if not addressed. Work through the techniques and exercises in this chapter and see how you can improve it.

3–4: Your memory for names and faces is average. Use the techniques and exercises in this chapter to boost your performance.
5–6: Your memory for names and faces is impressive. Stretch yourself to the limit with the tests in this chapter.

1 FUNNY FACES

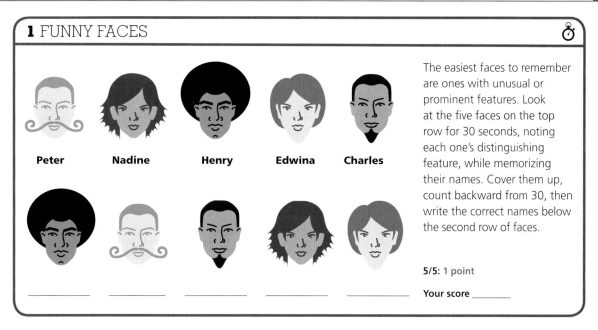

Peter   **Nadine**   **Henry**   **Edwina**   **Charles**

The easiest faces to remember are ones with unusual or prominent features. Look at the five faces on the top row for 30 seconds, noting each one's distinguishing feature, while memorizing their names. Cover them up, count backward from 30, then write the correct names below the second row of faces.

5/5: 1 point

Your score _____

_____   _____   _____   _____   _____

2 UNFUNNY FACES

Remembering less unusual faces can be much harder. Here is an exercise to help give a baseline for your performance in the rest of the chapter. Give yourself 1 minute to learn the names and faces on the top row. Cover them and spell out the months with fewer than 31 days, and then write the correct names below the bottom row of faces.

Finlay   **Kim**   **Abdul**   **Matthew**   **Annie**

_____   _____   _____   _____   _____

5/5: 2 points 4/5: 1 point   **Your score** _____

The simplest way to boost your memory for names is to repeat the name as soon as you hear it. This will help imprint the name into your brain for future recall. Another good way to work in repetition when you first meet someone is to reframe your introduction as a question. For instance, you might say, "Arthur Deeley was it? Is that spelled DEELEY or DEALEY?" Practice doing this each time you are introduced to somebody new.

TECHNIQUE: NAMES BY LOCATION

It can be useful to visualize a plan of who is positioned where and to remember their names according to their location. Imagine you have flown with a tour group to Barcelona, Spain. On the return journey, the tourists sit in the same seats on the plane, but they no longer have name badges. Use their positions on the seating plan below to help you memorize names for 1 minute, then cover it up. Wait another minute, then answer the questions below.

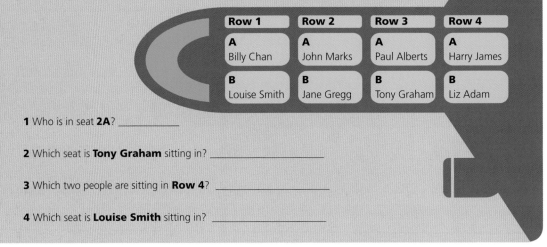

Row 1	Row 2	Row 3	Row 4
A Billy Chan	**A** John Marks	**A** Paul Alberts	**A** Harry James
B Louise Smith	**B** Jane Gregg	**B** Tony Graham	**B** Liz Adam

1 Who is in seat **2A**? _____

2 Which seat is **Tony Graham** sitting in? _____

3 Which two people are sitting in **Row 4**? _____

4 Which seat is **Louise Smith** sitting in? _____

3 GUEST HOUSE GUESSER

You have arrived at a guest house for the weekend with friends of your partner. Can you remember who is with whom and in which room each couple is staying? Memorize the list of couples and in which room they are staying for 1 minute, then cover the list and fill in the couples' names in the boxes on the room plan (right).

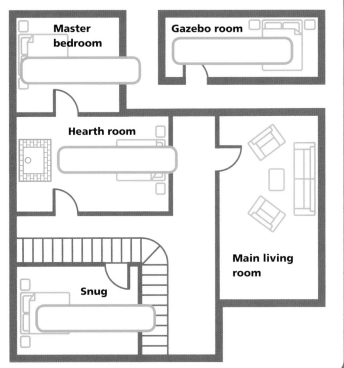

John and Jill are in the **Master bedroom**

Barbara and Kenneth are in the **Snug**

Lucy and Gokwan are in the **Hearth room**

Robert and Pamela are in the **Gazebo room**

Score 1 point for each couple placed correctly
Your score _____

4 DINNER PARTY CHALLENGE ⏱

You arrive late at a dinner party and your hostess makes a quick round of introductions. Study the list of names, faces, and seating positions below for 1 minute, then cover it up and take your seat at the table. Can you remember who is sitting where?

Martha, sitting on your right

Leo, sitting opposite you

Jeff, sitting on Leo's left

Andrew, sitting at the end nearest to you (on your left)

Louise, sitting at the far end of the table

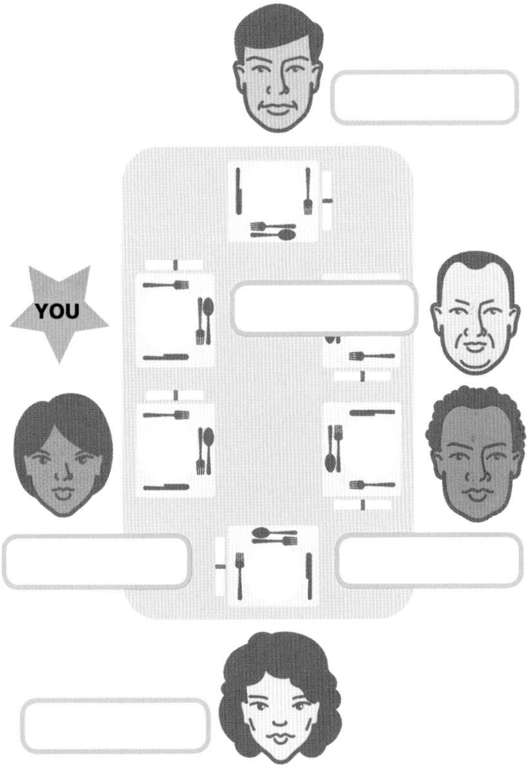

YOU

5 correct names/5: 1 point Your score _____

5 SCHOOL DAZE ⏱

It is your first day in a new class and the teacher asks you to distribute the papers he has just graded—but you've only had a short while to learn who is sitting where. Can you hand out each paper to the correct student? First study the seating plan below for 2 minutes, then cover it up and name 10 US states. Now write the names of the children in the blank spaces below.

Sarah	Frank	Julie
Jamilla	Henry	James
George	Samantha	Lucinda
Gary	Edward	You

1 _____ 2 _____ 3 _____

4 _____ 5 _____ 6 _____

7 _____ 8 _____ 9 _____

10 _____ 11 _____ You

11/11: 5 points 9–10/11: 4 points 7–8/11: 3 points
5–6/11: 2 points 3–4/11: 1 point Your score _____

6 ORDER ORDER

Recalling not just the names of people you have been introduced to but the order in which they were introduced might sound tricky, but if you can put the names into a simple but memorable narrative (a series of connected events), it could actually boost recall. Try to think of a narrative sequence with the characters below. After 2 minutes, cover up the names and faces, then name five James Bond films. Write down the names beneath the bottom row of faces and give the position each appeared in the sequence.

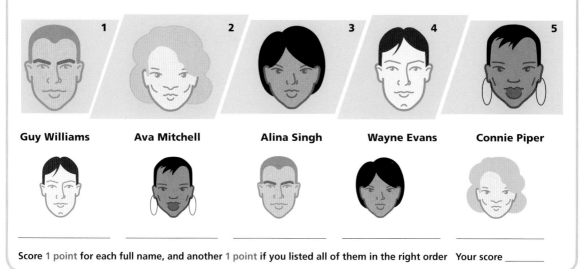

Score **1 point** for each full name, and another **1 point** if you listed all of them in the right order   Your score _____

7 NOMINATIVE DETERMINISM

When someone's job matches their name it is known as nominative determinism. It makes for a helpful mnemonic aid (a memory-enhancing technique). Memorize these names using their work association, cover, then list them:

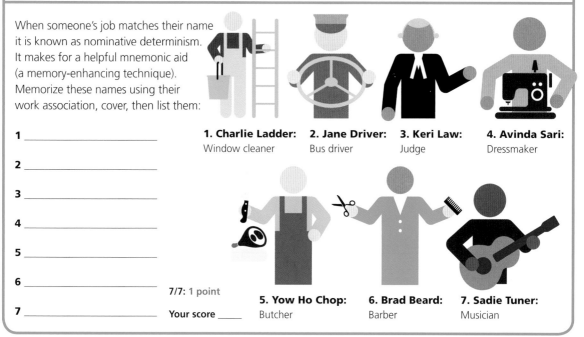

1 _____

2 _____

3 _____

4 _____

5 _____

6 _____

7 _____

1. Charlie Ladder: Window cleaner

2. Jane Driver: Bus driver

3. Keri Law: Judge

4. Avinda Sari: Dressmaker

5. Yow Ho Chop: Butcher

6. Brad Beard: Barber

7. Sadie Tuner: Musician

7/7: 1 point

Your score _____

TECHNIQUE: WHAT'S IN A NAME?

People with names that immediately suggest a visualization or association are a gift to someone who has a poor memory. For each of these four people, think of an obvious association or visualization. For instance, you might remember Mr. Butterman by visualizing him being spread on toast. Once you've got your memory cues for the other three names and faces, cover the names beneath the faces and see if you can use your visualizations to recall their names.

Mr. Butterman **Miss Plum** **Mr. Golightly** **Mrs. Atticus**

_____ _____ _____ _____

8 MEET THE INTERVIEW PANEL

You want to make a good impression at an interview, but everyone in the panel is dressed alike. Can you remember who is who? Using the technique above, try making a visualization or association with these less memorable names. Study the names above the panel for 30 seconds, then cover them up and recite every third letter of the alphabet. Now try to recall the names.

Mr. Poole **Ms. Nolan** **Mr. Basu** **Mr. Goodall** **Mrs. Hall**

_____ _____ _____ _____ _____

5/5: you're hired! 1 point   Your score _____

TECHNIQUE: MAKE IT MEMORABLE

Boost memory by using correspondences between names and a person's appearance. First, focus on an individual's features, then see if you can make a memorable visualization linking the features to the person's name. To practice this, give yourself 2 minutes to jot down on a separate piece of paper memorable visualizations linking each of these name/face combos. Then cover up the faces and your visualization, and see if you can recall the names.

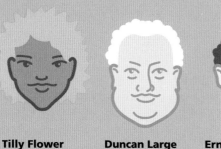

Tilly Flower   **Duncan Large**   **Ernest Monkton**   **Pepper Prado**   **Sampson Ching**

9 TRAIN CHARACTERS

To practice this technique, begin by just remembering people according to their features. Six unusual-looking passengers share your train car on a long trip. The next day you try to describe to a friend what they all looked like. Study the passengers below left, then cover them up and wait 5 minutes. Now write down the missing distinguishing features for the faces on the right.

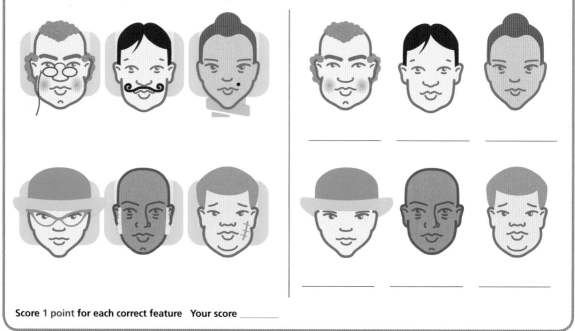

Score 1 point for each correct feature   Your score _____

10 IDENTIKIT

Now practice making associations between names and features with this exercise. Study the five pictures on top and memorize the features for each name, then cover them, name the titles of the last three books you read, then see if you can remember the name that goes with the face.

Polly Turner

Sunil Batra

Joe Seymour

Augustine Brown

Jade Pike

11 IF THE NAME FITS

Now combine names and features with a visualization. At Great-aunt Greta's 80th birthday party you can't remember the names of half your relatives. Your sister gives you a quick run down: give yourself 1 minute to connect these names and faces with visuals, then cover them up and, on the right, fill in the name below the relative, as well as drawing in their missing feature.

Score 1 point for each correct name and 1 point for each correct feature

Your score _____

Cousin Wade

Aunt Faith

Uncle Rupert   **Nephew William**   **Niece Ida**

12 COUPLING UP

If you find it difficult remembering people's names, then recalling the names of their partner may be even harder. Try using some of the techniques you've learned to memorize who is with whom. Below are four couples. Use their names or memorable features as the basis for associations, then cover them up. Move on to exercise 13, then come back to fill in the blanks on the right.

Who is **Celeste** with? _____

is with _____

Who is **Abdul** with? _____

is with _____

Who is **Felix** with? _____

is with _____

Harry and Meg

Celeste and Arthur

Abdul and Fatima

Ruby and Felix

6/6: 1 point   Your score _____

13 WE COME IN PEACE

This extra-tough challenge requires you to remember alien appearances and names. Aliens have landed and selected you to be Intergalactic Ambassador for Humanity. It is essential you follow protocol and remember each alien's name. Study the aliens and their names below for 2 minutes, cover them, and name the last five films you have watched. Then connect the names to the aliens pictured below.

Score 1 point for each alien's name you correctly recalled

Your score _____

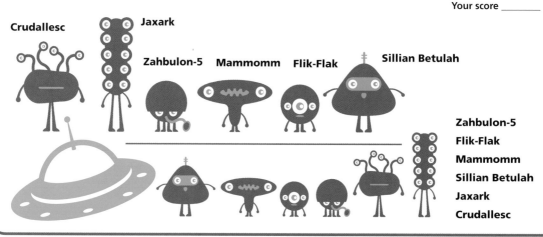

Crudallesc

Jaxark

Zahbulon-5   Mammomm   Flik-Flak   Sillian Betulah

Zahbulon-5
Flik-Flak
Mammomm
Sillian Betulah
Jaxark
Crudallesc

TECHNIQUE: CONTEXT IS KEY

By giving context to any new introduction you can help boost your recall. Pay attention to the circumstances around an introduction—where you were, what was in the background, what was the occasion, and so on. Use these examples as practice. Give yourself 2 minutes to learn them, name 12 European countries, then see if you can remember who is who.

Phillipa you met on a windy day

Vanessa you met on a visit to London

Ardal you met at a firework display

Imogen was carrying roses when you met

Nishit you met on a plane

14 TESTING TIMES

Can you remember the names of these school teachers and their subjects? Study the list for 1 minute, using the topics of the lessons and the classroom setting to forge a memorable visualization with each teacher's name. Then cover it all, complete exercise 15, and come back and see if you can write their names and subjects down below.

Mrs. Proud (History)

Mr. D'Angelo (Art)

Mr. Edwards (Geography)

Ms. Farnborough (Literature)

1 _____

2 _____

3 _____

4 _____

5 _____

6 _____

Score 1 point for each correct name

Your score _____

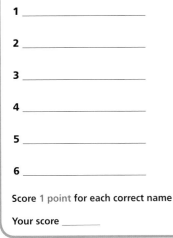
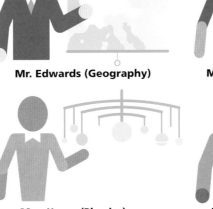

Mrs. Hwan (Physics)

Mr. Letterman (Biology)

Putting together some of the tips used in this chapter so far results in a technique called the three-step booster. This involves using a person's name to suggest one memorable association, using their facial features to suggest another association, and then combining the two to create an overall super-memorable association. In the example below, you can associate Linda Scott's name with a Scottie dog and her hair style with a beehive, then combine the two in a memorable image: the Scottie dog chasing bees. Can you do the same with David Hooper?

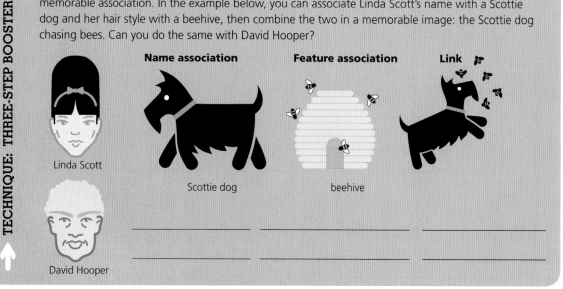

Name association

Feature association

Link

Linda Scott

Scottie dog

beehive

David Hooper

15 UNFORGETTABLE FACES

Use the three-step booster technique to memorize these four name–face combos. Think of an association for each name and then an association for each face, then link the two associations in a memorable image. Now cover the names, associations, and links and think of 12 types of birds. Then, on a separate piece of paper, see if you can write down the name that goes with each face.

		Name association	Face association	Link
Chavez	1			
Aminah	2			
Fion	3			
Fawcett	4			

Score 1 point for each name you remember   Your score _____

16 TRADE PLACES

You are sent to welcome a trading delegation from China, but your boss turns up and wants to be introduced to each person. You heard the guests' names only once and now you have to remember them or risk causing offense! Can you put your three-step booster technique to the ultimate test by rapidly forging robust visualizations after looking at the list of names and features only once? Cover the names and your links, name seven newspapers, and see if you can write down each guest's name on a separate piece of paper.

		Name association	Face association	Link
Wu Zhaoxu Head of the delegation	1			
Song Bingguo Assistant to Mr. Wu Zhaoxu	2			
Gao Lei Only woman in the delegation	3			
Qin Lingyu Translator	4			
Zhang We Director of Resources	5			

Score 2 points for each name you remember   Your score _____

Your score   **/75**   **60–75 GOLD**    **30–59 SILVER**   **0–29 BRONZE**

60–75 GOLD
You are brilliant at remembering names and faces, and are probably blessed with a good memory overall. Hone your skills by practicing techniques like the three-step booster.

30–59 SILVER
You could improve your memory for names and faces. Check out the Challenge on page 178 and keep working on your name–face associations.

0–29 BRONZE
You could be inconveniencing and embarrassing yourself with your poor memory for names and faces. Try the Challenge and then go back and work through the exercises, with special attention to the techniques.

★ Turn to page 178 for the Challenge.

CHAPTER 3
EVERYDAY ELEPHANT
EVERYDAY CHALLENGES

Everyday elephant

In the modern world there is a host of common tasks and data to remember—the sort of things our memories struggle to cope with. To master the mundane requires a special blend of short- and long-term memory boosters.

QUESTIONNAIRE

Complete this quick questionnaire to evaluate your baseline performance in this area.

1 Do you sometimes get to work and realize you've left your mobile phone at home?

Rarely/Sometimes/Often
[score 2 points for "Rarely," 1 for "Sometimes"]

2 Do you sometimes have to spend time hunting for your keys before you can leave the house?

Rarely/Sometimes/Often
[score 2 points for "Rarely," 1 for "Sometimes"]

3 At home your online journey planner sets out a walking route for you, but will you be able to remember the directions without a printout?

Likely/Unlikely
[score 1 point for "Likely"]

4 Do you sometimes return from shopping and realize you've bought everything except the thing you went out for?

Rarely/Sometimes/Often
[score 2 points for "Rarely," 1 for "Sometimes"]

5 The last time for sending international mail the next day has been announced. Will you remember to mail your letters?

Yes/No
[score 1 point for "Yes"]

6 Do you sometimes forget to take your shopping list to the supermarket?

Rarely/Sometimes/Often
[score 2 points for "Rarely," 1 for "Sometimes"]

How did you score?

0–3: Your memory for everyday tasks is weak. Fortunately this chapter is here to help—practice the techniques and work on the exercises.

4–7: Your memory for everyday tasks is average. Sharpen it by working on the exercises in this chapter.

8–10: You have a good memory for everyday tasks. This chapter will help you maintain this level of performance.

1 SHOPPING TEST

How much of your shopping can you remember without taking a list? Study the items on the right for 30 seconds. Now cover them up, list eight flowers, and then write down as many of the items as you can recall.

1 _____   5 _____

2 _____   6 _____

3 _____   7 _____

4 _____   8 _____

8/8: 1 point   Your score _____

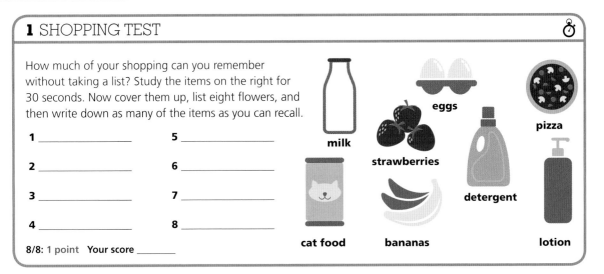

milk

eggs

strawberries

pizza

cat food

bananas

detergent

lotion

TECHNIQUE: MEMORY HOUSE SYSTEM

The memory house is a mnemonic device where you picture the layout of a house, place items on your list in the rooms, and create a memorable visual linking the item with the room. For example, in each room of the house shown below is a memorable association to an item on a shopping list: spaghetti, lamb chops, toilet paper, soap, tuna, and wine. Study the house for 2 minutes, then cover it, wait 5 minutes, and write the list on a separate piece of paper.

Attic: girl with spaghetti hair

Bedroom: lamb in bed

Bathroom: bubble bath in the tub

Living room: roll of toilet paper on sofa

Kitchen: tuna fishing

Cellar: gorilla collecting wine

---

2 MEMORY HOUSE

Practice the memory house system using the house below. Imagine the items from the list in the rooms in striking scenarios. Once you've finished, cover the house and list, and wait 2 minutes before trying to recall the list.

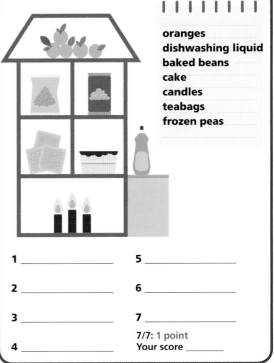

oranges
dishwashing liquid
baked beans
cake
candles
teabags
frozen peas

1 _____   5 _____

2 _____   6 _____

3 _____   7 _____

7/7: 1 point
Your score _____

4 _____

TECHNIQUE: LINK SYSTEM

The link system is another technique that uses strong imagery to make memorable associations. Items you want to remember are linked together in unusual and striking ways. Below is an example of how you might visualize, link, and remember three items on your shopping list.

On your shopping list you need to remember these three items: fish, bacon, bagels.

Step 1

Create a memorable image for each item: a fish with hands, bacon dancing, bagels as balloons.

Step 2

Now link the three images into one single memorable visualization: the fish holding the bagel balloons and dancing with the bacon.

3 LINK LOVIN'

Let's work on the link system some more. On your shopping list are lemons, chocolate, milk, bread, and carrots. Below is a memorable image for each of these—can you think of one memorable scenario linking all five items? Now cover the images, list eight South American countries, then try to remember your scenario and use it to recall the items on your list. Write them down on the note paper provided.

5/5: 1 point   Your score _____

4 LINK LIFE

You can also use the link system to remember lists of household chores or appointments. Write or sketch link visualizations for each set of images below, then cover them and come back 5 minutes later to test your recall for the link.

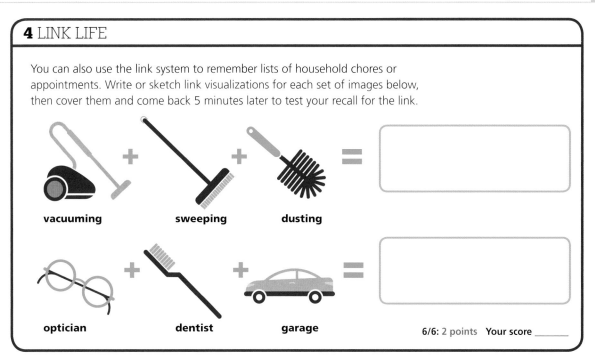

vacuuming + **sweeping** + **dusting** =

optician + **dentist** + **garage** =

6/6: 2 points   Your score _____

TECHNIQUE: ACRONYMS ASSEMBLE

An acronym is a word formed from the initial letters of a series of words. For example, WHO is an acronym for World Health Organization. You can use the initials of items on a list you need to remember to make a memorable acronym. Suppose an acronym of your shopping list spelled out TYGRR: you could then also use a tiger as the basis for a visualization. Try turning the initials of these items you need for a picnic into a memorable acronym.

plates, apples, basket, utensils, bread, cupcakes, wine, ice pack

5 ACRONYM ANTICS

Practice the acronym technique by using it to generate a memorable acronym for this list of things you need to get from the hardware store. Pick one that suggests a striking image, fix it in your mind, then cover the list. Write down eight vegetables and then try to recall the list.

hammer, primer, nails, glue, oil, file, tape measure, paint

8/8: 2 points **7/8:** 1 point

Your score _____

TECHNIQUE: ACROSTIC TACTICS

An acrostic is a phrase, verse, or sentence where the initial letters of each word on a list or in a sequence spell out a word to combine together into a sentence you can easily remember. You can then use this sentence (or acrostic) to remind you of the words you are trying to remember. For instance, Hurry Up The Beach is Lovely could stand for a list of things to take to the beach: hat, umbrella, towel, books, and lotion. Try making an acrostic to remind you of the ingredients you need for a cake:

flour, sugar, milk, butter, eggs, lemons, nutmeg

6 ACROSTIC SLEEPOVER

Your child is having a sleepover: make sure you don't forget anything by coming up with an acrostic for the items on the right. Then cover the items and your acrostic, name eight marine creatures, and then using your acrostic see if you can recall the items you need to remember for the sleepover.

1 _____

2 _____

3 _____

4 _____

5 _____

6 _____

7 _____

7/7: 2 points 6/7: 1 point

Your score _____

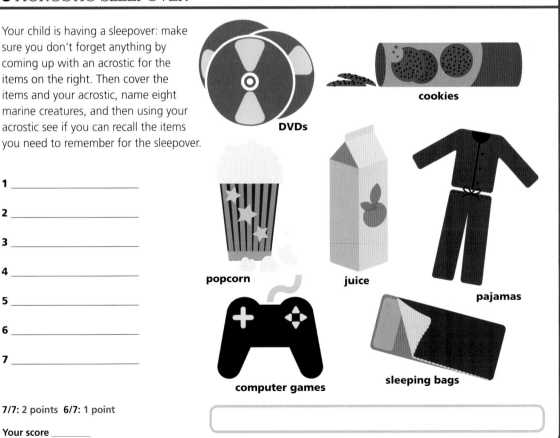

DVDs

cookies

popcorn

juice

pajamas

computer games

sleeping bags

7 ACROSTIC CHRISTMAS LIST

A relative has given you her Christmas wish list. Make sure you don't forget any of the gifts on the list by coming up with a memorable acrostic from an arrangement of the first letters of the items below. Cover the list and your acrostic, wait 5 minutes, and then try to recall the list.

DVD

novel

earrings

socks

smartphone

sweater

perfume

1 _____   5 _____

2 _____   6 _____

3 _____   7 _____

4 _____

7/7: 2 points 6/7: 1 point

Your score _____

8 TASKS CHECKLIST

You have a busy week ahead, so to help you remember the items on your "to do" list, see if you can come up with an acrostic from an arrangement of the first letters of each task below. Cover it up, list eight cartoon characters, and then see if you can recall the list.

theater trip

dry cleaning

children's party

doctor

abc

parents' evening

team meeting

window cleaner

1 _____   5 _____

2 _____   6 _____

3 _____   7 _____

4 _____

7/7: 2 points 6/7: 1 point

Your score _____

A peg system is a mnemonic where you create a series of striking images that you know by heart (your "pegs"). You can create a visualization linking your pegs to the things that you need to remember (such as the items on a shopping list or a list of household chores). The theory is that because you already know your pegs, it is easy to recall the visualizations linked to them and therefore you can remember the items on the list. Once you have formed and memorized your peg images, you have a widely applicable toolkit for use in forming memorable imagery-based associations with items on any list you need to remember. There are many possible peg systems. Here, the alphabet peg system is shown and pegs have been created for the first three letters of the alphabet. Follow the steps and see if you can come up with your own memorable pegs for the whole alphabet.

Items to remember:
oranges
pasta
cheese

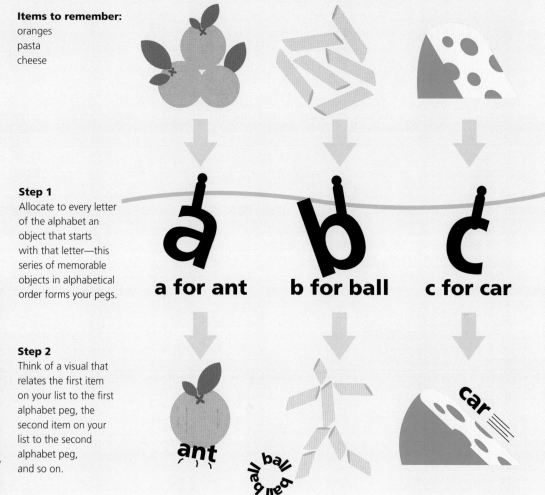

TECHNIQUE: ALPHABET PEG SYSTEM

Step 1
Allocate to every letter of the alphabet an object that starts with that letter—this series of memorable objects in alphabetical order forms your pegs.

a for ant   b for ball   c for car

Step 2
Think of a visual that relates the first item on your list to the first alphabet peg, the second item on your list to the second alphabet peg, and so on.

Step 3
When you need to remember a list, work through your alphabet pegs and each respective visualization to help you recall the items on it. The key is to learn your alphabet pegs; then visualizations should be easily recalled.

9 ALPHABET PEG PRACTICE

Use your own alphabet pegs to memorize the items you need to pack for a vacation. For instance, if your peg for "d" is "dog" you could imagine the corresponding item on the list—your passport—open to the photo page with a passport photo of a dog. Try applying the alphabet peg system to the whole list on the right, then cover it, wait 5 minutes, and see if you can recall all the items in order.

money
tickets
travel guide
passport
sunglasses
sun cream
flip flops
toothbrush
camera
phrase book

1 _____
2 _____
3 _____
4 _____
5 _____
6 _____
7 _____
8 _____
9 _____
10 _____

10/10: 2 points **8–9:** 1 point **Your score** _____

10 MORE ALPHABET PEG PRACTICE

Practice your alphabet peg technique again by using it to memorize a list of sights you want to see when you visit Sydney. For instance, if your peg for "c" is "car," create a visual in your head for the corresponding item on your list—perhaps the fish in the aquarium (representing Sydney Aquarium) driving a car. Try this for the whole list below, cover it, name five Australian cities, then try to recall all the sights in order.

1 _____
2 _____
3 _____
4 _____
5 _____
6 _____
7 _____
8 _____
9 _____
10 _____

Sydney Opera House
Royal Botanic Gardens
Sydney Aquarium
Museum of Contemporary Art
Sydney Harbour Bridge

The Rocks
Taronga Zoo
Circular Quay
Batemans Bay
Jenolan Caves

10/10: 2 points **8–9:** 1 point **Your score** _____

TECHNIQUE: RHYMING NUMBER PEGS

Another peg system you can apply to help everyday memory of lists and tasks is the rhyming number peg system. Here, your pegs are numbers instead of letters. Attached to each number peg is a word that rhymes with that number. You can then associate the things on your list to your rhyming pegs.

Items to remember:
oranges
pasta
cheese

Step 1
Think of a word that rhymes with the number of the peg. For example, 1 could be sun, 2 could be shoe, 3 could be sea, and so on.

Step 2
Relate each item on your list to the corresponding peg number. So, if the first thing on your list is oranges, apply oranges to the number 1 peg by linking the item to the rhyming word to create a memorable image. For example, you could visualize an orange as the sun. Do the same with the rest of the items on the list.

Step 3
When you need to remember your list, work through your rhyming number pegs and their associated visuals to help you recall the items on it.

11 RHYMING NUMBER PEG PRACTICE

Practice your rhyming number peg system by applying it to a list of household chores. Assign the chores to your number rhymes in sequence, making striking associations. For instance, if your rhyme for "8" is "plate," you could visualize a clean bathtub full of plates. When you've visualized the whole list, cover it and wait 5 minutes. Now try to recall the list of chores in order.

wash kitchen floor
take out garbage
clean refrigerator
empty recycling
fill up salt shaker
mow lawn
change sheets
clean bathtub

1 _____

2 _____

3 _____

4 _____

5 _____

6 _____

7 _____

8 _____

8/8: 2 points **7/8:** 1 point

Your score _____

12 CHUNK THAT LIST

As we saw in Chapter 1, chunking—splitting items into related groups—is a handy shortcut for remembering things. Previously, you sorted the items into pairs. Now, group items into categories of more than two. Divide these school items into three groups based on where the items will go—sports bag, lunch box, and school bag. Cover it up, name eight insects, and then try to recall the list, writing each item in the relevant place.

sneakers
socks
racket
sweatband
apple
fruit juice
sandwich
grapes
homework
textbooks
pencil case
calculator

12/12: 2 points 10–11: 1 point

Your score _____

13 SUPERMARKET SWEEP

Another way of chunking is to divide a shopping list according to the aisles of the supermarket you will need to visit. Assign each of these items to the relevant aisle at the supermarket—fruit and vegetables, freezer, or drinks—then cover the list and name eight breeds of dog. Then try to remember the list by recalling which aisle you will find each item on.

lemonade
potato chips
grapes
bottled water
potatoes
ice cream
leeks
apple cider
ice cubes
lager
watermelon
frozen shrimp

12/12: 2 points 10–11: 1 point Your score _____

14 MOON STREET

Remembering directions can be difficult and it can help to use the names of streets to suggest memorable images. Try memorizing this list of directions, then cover and retest yourself after waiting 5 minutes.

Left at **Nightingale Avenue**

Straight on at **Moon Street**

Right at **Floral Lane**

Right again at **Farm Fields**

Straight on down
Frenchman's Row

Left at **The Cut**

Right at **Wall Street**

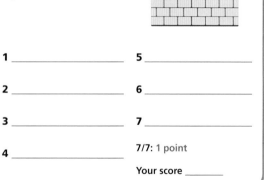

1 _____   5 _____

2 _____   6 _____

3 _____   7 _____

4 _____   **7/7: 1 point**

Your score _____

15 COMPASS ROSE

Add to your direction visualization a system for remembering left–right orientation. For instance, a system based on a compass that equates West with an appropriate image (such as a cowboy) and uses that as a mnemonic image for left. East becomes right, North means go straight on and South means double back. Can you come up with images for these?

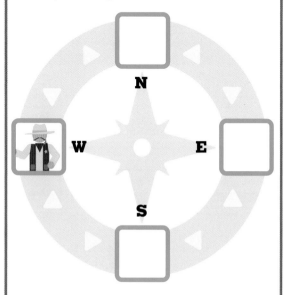

Now try combining this system with images suggested by place names in this sequence of directions. Once you have an image for each direction, cover the list and write your name backward. Now see if you can recall all five directions using the images you created.

1 Turn left onto Tower Street
2 Go straight across at the junction with Hangman's Hill
3 Turn right onto Cloudman's Road
4 Turn left onto Weasley Gardens
5 Go straight across at St. Paul's Square

1 _____   4 _____

2 _____   5 _____

3 _____   **5/5: 1 point**

Your score _____

16 LEFT AND RIGHT

A flurry of directions can be hard to remember. Turn the lefts and rights into an acrostic by combining pairs of directions into the basis for words. For instance, left followed by right (LR) becomes **LiRa**. Right followed by right (RR) becomes **RoaRing**. Try turning the directions into words with the series of directions below, then cover the directions, list eight clothing items, and trace out a path on the grid beginning at "start."

Right, left; Left, right; Right, left; Right, right

Where did you end up? _____

Answer on page 180

Right place: score 1 point   Your score _____

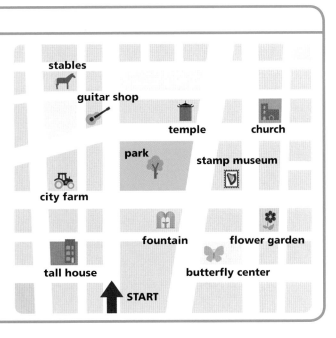

17 CHECKPOINTS

Chunking is a great technique for making a long set of directions easier to remember. Essentially this means breaking down your journey into sections, like following a series of checkpoints. So, rather than remembering how to get all the way from Berry Road to Garfield Place, you remember how to get from Berry Road to C Street, then C Street to Jefferson Square, and so on. Chunk this list, then cover it and try to navigate the map.

1 East on Berry Road
2 Fourth right onto Brick Lane
3 First right onto C Street
4 Cross over the intersection
5 Turn left onto Diwan Avenue
6 Second right into Jefferson Square
7 Across the square and up Sharma Heights
8 Third right onto Garfield Place

How many directions did you remember? 8/8: 2 points 7/8: 1 point   Your score _____

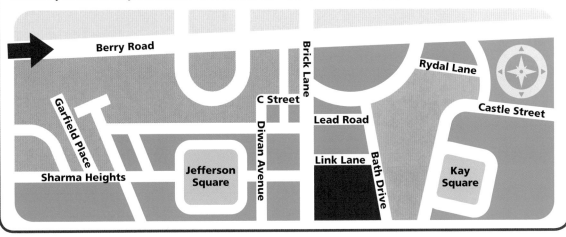

18 KEY FINDER

Remembering, let alone finding, your keys is an everyday challenge for many people. Test your key memory with this quick quiz: where are these keys right now?

1 _____

2 _____

3 _____

4 _____

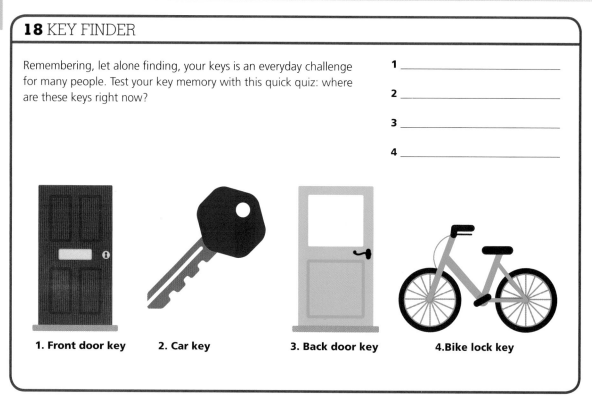

1. Front door key   **2. Car key**   **3. Back door key**   **4. Bike lock key**

19 KEYS TO THE KINGDOM

Improve your memory for key location by building striking associations between each key and where you keep it. Below are four images to help you remember four different locations. Visualize them for 30 seconds, cover them, name eight rivers, then try to remember where all four keys are.

1 _____

2 _____

3 _____

4 _____

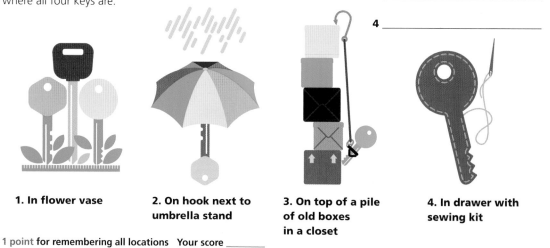

1. In flower vase   **2. On hook next to umbrella stand**   **3. On top of a pile of old boxes in a closet**   **4. In drawer with sewing kit**

1 point for remembering all locations   Your score _____

20 KEY CREATIVITY

Try coming up with your own visual locations for keys. Here are four locations—for each one write or sketch a memorable visual link. Then cover and come back after counting up your score so far for this chapter. Can you remember all four locations?

1 _____

2 _____

3 _____

4 _____

2. In jar on kitchen counter

1. On top of frame of door leading onto garden

3. In drawer in hall cabinet with passports and foreign currency

4. On hook by front door next to boots and shoes

4/4: 1 point Your score _____

TIP

Make a home for your keys. If you always put your keys in the same place you will never have to look for them! Pick a good spot—for example, a hook in the hallway—and make a point of always hanging your keys there when you come in. If you forget, go back and do it as soon as you remember. Soon it will become a habit and your keys will never be lost again.

Your score   **/40**

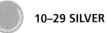 **30–40 GOLD**

Impressive—your memory is in good shape for everyday tasks. Keep practicing visualization and association skills to keep up the high level of performance.

 **10–29 SILVER**

Your memory is average when it comes to everyday tasks. Check out the Challenge on page 178, and go back and work on some of the tips.

 0–9 BRONZE

Poor memory hampers your performance on everyday tasks. Try out the Challenge and then go back and work through the puzzles agan.

 Turn to page 178 for the Challenge

CHAPTER 4
WHERE'S MY CAR?
MEDIUM-TERM MEMORY

Where's my car?

Somewhere between short- and long-term memory is a stage where information is being laid down, but is not yet fully encoded. This is medium-term memory (MTM). Anything you have remembered for more than a minute but less than a week fits into this category.

QUESTIONNAIRE
Use this quick quiz to get an instant rating of your MTM skills.

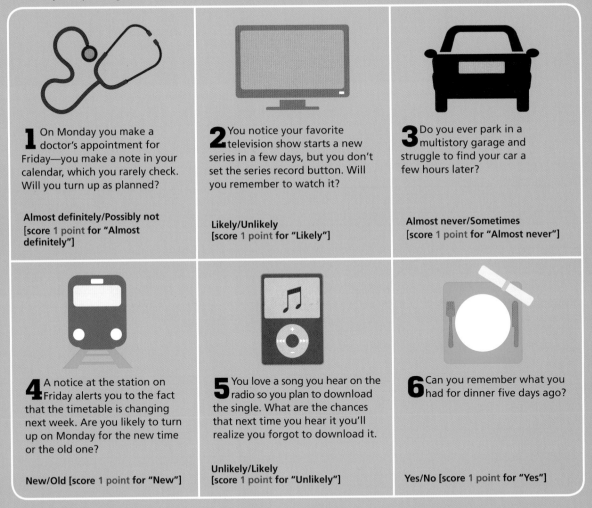

1 On Monday you make a doctor's appointment for Friday—you make a note in your calendar, which you rarely check. Will you turn up as planned?

Almost definitely/Possibly not [score 1 point for "Almost definitely"]

2 You notice your favorite television show starts a new series in a few days, but you don't set the series record button. Will you remember to watch it?

Likely/Unlikely [score 1 point for "Likely"]

3 Do you ever park in a multistory garage and struggle to find your car a few hours later?

Almost never/Sometimes [score 1 point for "Almost never"]

4 A notice at the station on Friday alerts you to the fact that the timetable is changing next week. Are you likely to turn up on Monday for the new time or the old one?

New/Old [score 1 point for "New"]

5 You love a song you hear on the radio so you plan to download the single. What are the chances that next time you hear it you'll realize you forgot to download it?

Unlikely/Likely [score 1 point for "Unlikely"]

6 Can you remember what you had for dinner five days ago?

Yes/No [score 1 point for "Yes"]

How did you score?
0–2: A poor MTM means you are likely to be forgetting things from one day to the next, which is possibly trying. There are lots of tips in this chapter to help you.
3–4: Your MTM is average, which means you would benefit from improvements. Work through the exercises in this chapter, paying close attention to the techniques, and see how you do.
5–6: Your MTM is strong, and you are unlikely to miss appointments, forget arrangements, or lose cars. Hone your abilities with these exercises, and practice new strategies to maintain your MTM performance.

1 CALL HISTORY

A good way to stretch your MTM is to see if you can recall (without electronic aids) the people who called you most recently on your mobile phone. List the names of your last five callers below.

1 _____

2 _____

3 _____

4 _____

5 _____

Score 1 point for each caller remembered

Your score _____

2 DINNER DIARY

A good test of MTM is whether you can recall what you ate for dinner recently. Can you fill in this dinner diary?

What did you have for dinner...

yesterday _____ Score 1 point

2 days ago _____ Score 1 point

3 days ago _____ Score 1 point

4 days ago _____ Score 1 point

5 days ago _____ Score 2 points

Your score _____

3 AD BUSTER

Stretch your MTM some more by seeing if you can remember advertisements you have seen on television. When watching TV, write down the first five advertisements you see, then see if you can recall them at the same time the next day.

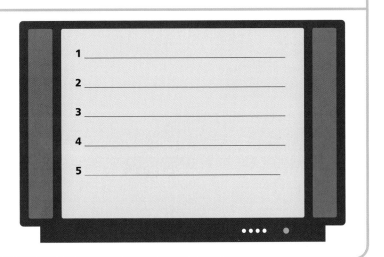

1 _____

2 _____

3 _____

4 _____

5 _____

Score 1 point for each advertisement you remembered

Your score _____

The journey method is a peg system to help you remember things on a list. The stages of a journey (either real-life or fictional) are the pegs. Once you have decided on your journey and its various stages, you can then link each stage to an item on your list by creating a visualization linking the two. Below, for example, the first stage of a journey is passing the gates of horn, which are guarded by griffons—this is your peg to which you link the first item you need to remember on your list. Practice is key with the journey method, so to begin, try to remember these six fantasy journey stages as your pegs, and recall them after 5 minutes.

1 The gates of horn, guarded by griffons

2 The forest of fear, infested by goblins

3 The meadow of sleep, full of poppies

4 The bottomless chasm, crossed by a rope bridge

5 The fortress of bronze, with a custard moat

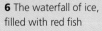

6 The waterfall of ice, filled with red fish

TECHNIQUE: JOURNEY METHOD

4 JOURNEY METHOD PRACTICE

Use your journey pegs (either your own or the example journey, left) to remember the six tasks listed below. For each one, a striking visual link between the item and the journey stage has been made. For example, for "pick up grammy," the first item, you could imagine grammy being carried away by a griffon. When you've understood and memorized the visualizations, cover the list, name eight types of fruit, then see how many of the tasks on the list you can remember.

1 Pick up grammy

2 Call dentist

3 Get present

4 Get tires checked

5 Call Barbara

6 Water houseplants

1 _____   **4** _____

2 _____   **5** _____

3 _____   **6** _____

6/6: 1 point

Your score _____

5 CAR PARK PANIC

Use the journey method to memorize where you have parked your car. Once you've made your visualizations, cover the list, and come back in 5 minutes and locate the correct bay.

You parked in: **Green level, Area E, Bay 13**

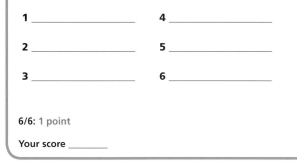

Correct bay remembered: 1 point   Your score _____

6 THERE AND BACK AGAIN

You've just started a new job and you need to learn the new commute. Use the journey method to help you remember the landmarks along the route. Cover the list of landmarks, name eight birds, then try to recall your new route.

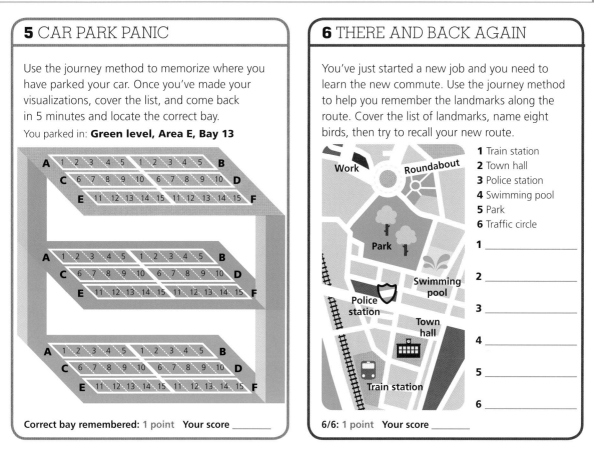

1 Train station
2 Town hall
3 Police station
4 Swimming pool
5 Park
6 Traffic circle

1 _____

2 _____

3 _____

4 _____

5 _____

6 _____

6/6: 1 point   Your score _____

7 FLOOR PLAN

You could also use the rooms of a multistory building, such as a college dormitory, for your journey pegs. Imagine you are a student and have to remember the list of textbooks you need to buy for your courses. Create a memorable visualization between the room and the book titles. Cover the list of textbooks, name eight Disney films, then see if you can recall the titles.

1 _____   **4** _____

2 _____   **5** _____

3 _____   **6** _____

6/6: 1 point

Your score _____

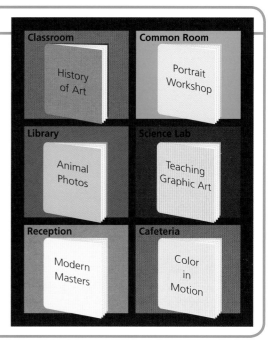

Classroom — History of Art
Common Room — Portrait Workshop
Library — Animal Photos
Science Lab — Teaching Graphic Art
Reception — Modern Masters
Cafeteria — Color in Motion

TECHNIQUE: DAYS OF THE WEEK PEG SYSTEM

The days of the week make another good basis for a peg system. The pegs are the individual days (Monday, Tuesday, and so on), and each peg is linked to a memorable visual. The visual could, for example, be something that stems from the word itself, such as the spelling, look, or pronunciation of the word. You could link Monday to the moon; Tuesday to twins ("two sounds similar to "Tue"); Wednesday to a wedding cake (the "wed" of Wednesday); Thursday to a hammer (the shape of a capital "T"); Friday to a frying pan (the pronunciation of "Fri"); Saturday to a chair (you have "sat" in a chair); and Sunday to the sun. Once you have learned your visuals for each peg, you can then use them to help you remember events taking place on a particular day in the week ahead. Think of a visualization linking the event you need to remember to the day on which it occurs. For example, if you have a geography examination on Tuesday, you could think of an image with twins holding the Earth. Memorize your own pegs, or the ones given here, before trying the following puzzles.

MONDAY — Violin lesson

TUESDAY — Geography exam

WEDNESDAY — Tennis match

THURSDAY — Visit library

FRIDAY — Theater club

8 CLASS TIME

Imagine you've just started a new year at school. Classes begin every morning at 9am, but can you remember which class to turn up for first on which day? Use the weekday peg system above to create visualizations for which lesson takes place on which day. List eight mountains, then test yourself.

Mon: History
Tue: Spanish
Wed: Chemistry
Thu: Biology
Fri: Economics

Timetable

Mon _____

Tue _____

Wed _____

Thu _____

Fri _____

4/4: 1 point   Your score _____

TIP

An exercise to stretch your MTM into long term is to take a trip in your mind's eye down a street or route that you know well—your route home from work, for example. Try to remember and visualize all the major landmarks on the way, and estimate the time it takes to walk between them. Name the streets, stores, and natural features you go past. Try to make your visualization as detailed as possible, with colors, textures, sounds, and smells.

9 DAYS OF THE WEEK PEG PRACTICE

It is Sunday evening and you need to remember various activities taking place on specific days in the coming week. Use your days of the week pegs to create visualizations to help you remember what is taking place on which day. On Monday morning, see if you can remember your itinerary for the week.

Mon: Meeting with architects
Tue: Choosing carpets
Wed: Soccer match

Thu: Pick up boss from airport
Fri: Deadline for report

Sat: Going to the theater
Sun: Family lunch

Mon _____

Tue _____

Wed _____

Thu _____

Fri _____

Sat _____

Sun _____

7/7: **2 points** 6/7: **1 point**   **Your score** _____

10 INTERVIEW WEEK

You can use memorable aspects of an appointment itself to make striking associations with your weekday pegs. You have five different interviews set up. Work through the names on the right and assign associations between the names and your pegs. Cover them up and after 5 minutes see if you can remember who you are seeing on which day and the company's name.

Mon _____

Tue _____

Wed _____

Thu _____

Fri _____

5/5: **2 points** 4/5: **1 point**   **Your score** _____

Monday: Brenda at **Black Lagoon Ltd.**

Wednesday: Tariq at **Banner House**

Tuesday: Darren at **Tower Lights**

Thursday: Phillip at **Shell Place**

Friday: Ellie at **Berry & Sons**

For remembering specific times, or just as a generic peg system, a clock-face-based series of pegs is useful. Here the pegs are the hour numbers on a clock. Each peg is linked to a memorable visualization relating to that number or to the position on the clock face. For example, the hour 12 on the clock face ties in with North, or the hour 4 can be linked to a square, which has four sides. You then create a visualization between the hour peg of the appointment time you need to remember and the actual appointment. For example, if you needed to remember a doctor's appointment for 12 o'clock, you could visualize a needle pointing North. See if you can commit to memory these example hour visualizations, and also try to come up with your own version. Cover the clocks and name eight American states. Now test your memory of the pegs.

TECHNIQUE: CLOCK PEG SYSTEM

11 CALENDAR TREK

Can you use the clock peg system to memorize these seven appointments? Study them for 2 minutes, and when you're finished, cover them up, and think of five dinosaurs. Now fill in the blank diary spaces on the right.

9am: Marketing team meeting

10am: Sales pitch

11am: Quarterly results due

12am: TV interview

2pm: Partners' meeting

3pm: Interview receptionist candidates

4pm: Team drinks

9am _____

10am _____

11am _____

12am _____

2pm _____

3pm _____

4pm _____

7/7: 2 points
6/7: 1 point

Your score _____

12 NOW SHOWING

You're trying to plan a night at the movies but you only get a quick glance at the showing times for your local movie theaters. Can you memorize which film is on at what time and where, in less than 2 minutes? Then cover the list, think of five dog breeds, and test your recall.

5pm: The Red Rose at the Film House

7pm: Santa vs Aliens at the Roxy

8pm: Lords of the Air at the Empire

11pm: Too Many Cooks at the Curzon

Score 1 point for each showing time you correctly recalled Your score _____

13 MEDICATION MNEMONIC

A course of medication can involve a complicated timetable for taking pills. Use a clock peg system to help. Study the schedule below for 1 minute, cover it, write down your five favorite movies, then test yourself.

Blue pill:
11am and 4pm   _____

Red pill:
2pm   _____

Eye drops:
8am, 12pm, 4pm   _____

Green capsule:
9am and 6pm   _____

Score 1 point for each medication you correctly recalled Your score _____

14 PROGRAM REMINDER

Combining clock and weekday pegs can ensure than you never miss your favorite TV show again. For example, if you want to remember to watch a soap opera, and it is on at 7pm every Monday, you could visualize the sun setting (your hour peg for 7 o'clock) over the moon (your weekday peg for Monday). Look at the schedule of programs below for 2 minutes and combine your visualizations for the weekday and hour, then cover them all. List five green vegetables, then test your recall of the programs and the times they are showing.

Mondays 8pm:
Family Circle

Tuesdays 7pm:
Horse World

Wednesdays 8am:
Global News

Thursdays 9pm:
Birdwatch America

Saturdays 10am:
The Chef Show

Sundays 2pm:
Eden Gardens

1 _____

2 _____

3 _____

4 _____

5 _____

6 _____

6/6: 2 points
5/6: 1 point

Your score _____

15 FESTIVAL FUN TIMES

You're at a music festival and you don't want to miss any of your favorite bands. Using the combined clock and weekday peg system, memorize the line-up, then list five radio stations, before writing down which band is on when.

Fri 2pm: Berry Heads   **Fri 8pm:** Terrific Cones   **Sat 6pm:** The Bandannas

Sat 9pm: Honey Badger   **Sun 8pm:** Susie Spade   **Sun Midnight:** Argento Gents

1 _____

2 _____

3 _____

4 _____

5 _____

6 _____

6/6: 2 points
5/6: 1 point

Your score _____

16 OLYMPIC ROUNDUP

There's a big week of Olympic sport action ahead and you want to make sure you don't miss your favorite events. Using your combined clock and weekday peg system, can you memorize which sports are on when? Study the sports and times below for 1 minute, then cover them and name five ball sports before testing your recall.

Friday 9am:
Men's 200m hurdles

Wednesday 10.30am:
Men's tennis

Thursday 1pm:
Women's 100m swimming

Thursday 6pm:
Women's shotput

Monday 11am:
Women's archery

 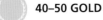

Sunday 7pm:
Men's heavyweight judo

1 _____

2 _____

3 _____

4 _____

5 _____

6 _____

6/6: 1 point

Your score _____

17 CRUISE CONTROL

There are lots of onboard events and activities offered during your week-long cruise vacation, and you don't want to miss any of them. Can you memorize the timetable below using the combined clock and weekday peg system? Give yourself 2 minutes of memorizing, then name five seas, and test for recall.

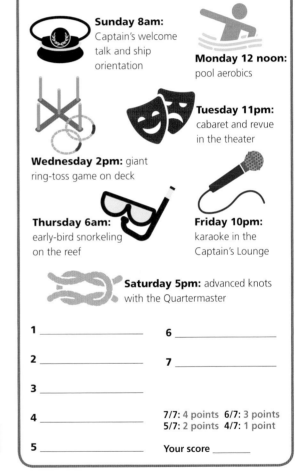

Sunday 8am:
Captain's welcome talk and ship orientation

Monday 12 noon:
pool aerobics

Tuesday 11pm:
cabaret and revue in the theater

Wednesday 2pm: giant ring-toss game on deck

Thursday 6am:
early-bird snorkeling on the reef

Friday 10pm:
karaoke in the Captain's Lounge

Saturday 5pm: advanced knots with the Quartermaster

1 _____

2 _____

3 _____

4 _____

5 _____

6 _____

7 _____

7/7: 4 points **6/7:** 3 points
5/7: 2 points **4/7:** 1 point

Your score _____

Your score   /50

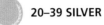 **40–50 GOLD**

Your MTM is well prepared for the challenges of everyday life, and if you can make a habit of practicing some of the tips and strategies covered in this chapter, your MTM will stay in top condition.

20–39 SILVER

You've given your MTM a good workout but you could benefit from improvements in all areas. Read the Challenge on page 178, and go back and try again the exercises where you struggled.

0–19 BRONZE

Your MTM is causing you problems. Try the Challenge on page 178, and go back and work through the exercises again.

 Turn to page 178 for the Challenge.

CHAPTER 5
I KNOW WHAT I DID
LAST SUMMER
LONG-TERM MEMORY

I know what I did last summer

Long-term memory (LTM) comes in many forms: memory of events that have happened in your life is known as biographical memory; recall of isolated facts requires semantic memory; and knowledge of skills, such as tying your shoelaces, is known as procedural memory.

QUESTIONNAIRE
Use this quick quiz to get an instant readout of your LTM status.

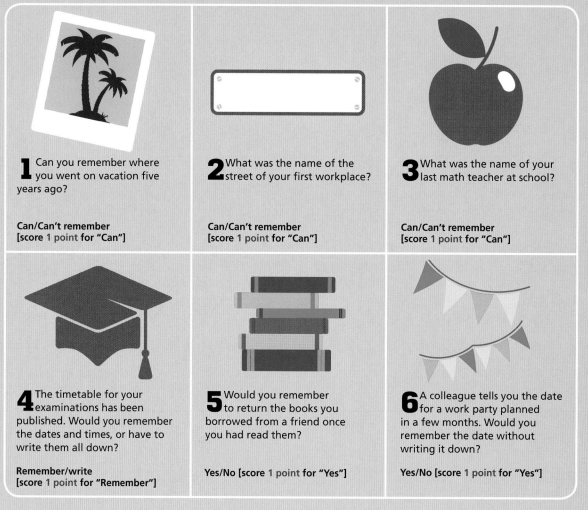

1 Can you remember where you went on vacation five years ago?

Can/Can't remember
[score 1 point for "Can"]

2 What was the name of the street of your first workplace?

Can/Can't remember
[score 1 point for "Can"]

3 What was the name of your last math teacher at school?

Can/Can't remember
[score 1 point for "Can"]

4 The timetable for your examinations has been published. Would you remember the dates and times, or have to write them all down?

Remember/write
[score 1 point for "Remember"]

5 Would you remember to return the books you borrowed from a friend once you had read them?

Yes/No [score 1 point for "Yes"]

6 A colleague tells you the date for a work party planned in a few months. Would you remember the date without writing it down?

Yes/No [score 1 point for "Yes"]

How did you score?
0–2: Your biographical memory is weak. The exercises in this chapter will help you expand your memory, and the techniques will help you improve it in the future.
3–4: You have an average biographical memory, which nevertheless means you could be forgetting important episodes. Work through the chapter to get a clearer picture of your strengths and gaps.
5–6: Your biographical memory is excellent; you should enjoy completing the exercises in this chapter, and along the way you may pick up tips to help keep this faculty in top condition.

1 WONDER YEARS

Despite what some people claim, everyone suffers from childhood amnesia: the loss of memories from the earliest years, before around age three to four. Let's probe the limits of your memory. In the spaces below, write down your five earliest memories.

2 TIMELINE

Let's go for a trip down memory lane with this timeline of life events. For each one rate your recall on a scale of 0 (it's a blank!) to 5 (total recall). Work out your overall score based on the categories you answered.

Recall

_____	First day at primary school
_____	Homeroom
_____	Starting at high school
_____	First date
_____	Exam results in last year of college
_____	Passing the road test for your driver license
_____	Graduation
_____	First job
_____	Wedding
_____	Moving into first family home
_____	Birth of first child
_____	Retirement

Total recall score _____

To work out your overall grading, multiply your total recall score by 10. Then add up the number of categories you answered and multiply this by 5. Now divide the first answer by the second to work out the number of points you scored out of 10.

Your score _____

3 FAMILY TREE

Your family history is an important part of your biographical makeup. Using the family tree below as an example, push your biographical memory to the limit by creating your own family tree on a separate piece of paper and seeing how far back you can go.

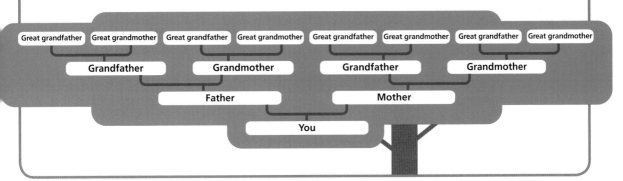

TECHNIQUE: EXPLORE THE SENSES

Even people for whom the biographical past is difficult to remember can find that once they start exploring their memories, things come flooding back. A useful strategy is to explore a memory one sense at a time. What could you smell? Were there any background noises? And so on. Below are some illustrated examples. Can you come up with your own sensory memories for these two travel experiences?

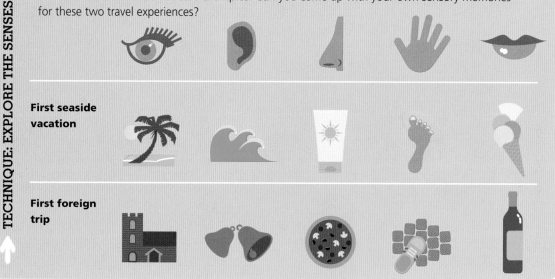

First seaside vacation

First foreign trip

4 POSTCARDS FROM THE PAST

Can you fill in your sensory memories for these events?

last vacation	last road trip	18th birthday	last restaurant visit

For each event, score **2 points** if you filled in 5/5 categories, **1 point** if you filled in 4/5   Your score _____

It can be difficult to remember the names of old acquaintances and distant relatives. Use this technique to help boost your memory when you meet up with people again in years to come. Use a familiar cast of characters from a well-known story and create memorable visualizations linking the faces and names to the characters. Try out this example using Snow White and the Seven Dwarfs to memorize the names of five friends. Create a memorable image for each, linking the individual to one of the characters, then cover the faces and after 5 minutes, recall your visualizations and see if you can remember the five names.

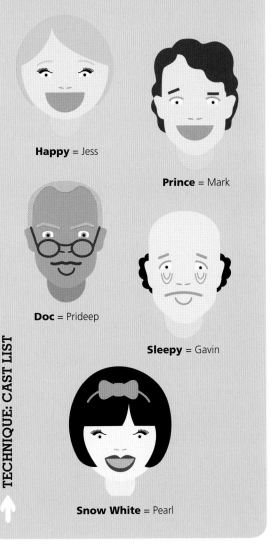

Happy = Jess

Prince = Mark

Doc = Prideep

Sleepy = Gavin

Snow White = Pearl

TECHNIQUE: CAST LIST

5 CASTING CALL

Can you come up with your own cast of characters to use as a visualization? For instance, you could use characters from famous films or books or comics. Using a lineup of your own invention, take 3 minutes to link the names and features of the people below to characters in your cast. Then test your recall of their names after listing five farm animals.

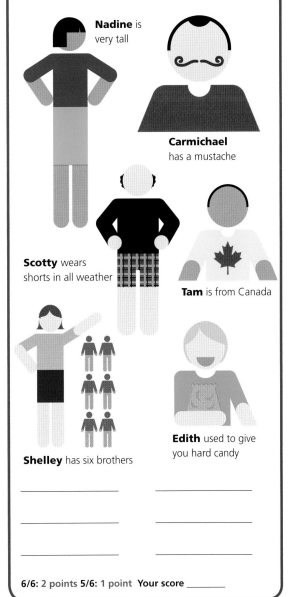

Nadine is very tall

Carmichael has a mustache

Scotty wears shorts in all weather

Tam is from Canada

Shelley has six brothers

Edith used to give you hard candy

_____ _____

_____ _____

_____ _____

6/6: 2 points 5/6: 1 point Your score _____

When you commit dates and appointments to memory, it is similar to committing any other isolated fact to memory, and this uses your semantic memory. As with other peg systems, calendar pegs help boost encoding and recall of semantic memory through use of vivid, memorable, and accessible images.

The months of the year make good pegs because they are a familiar sequence and help with recall of dates and appointments. Here are some suggested peg images for the months of the year relating to the season/name of the month itself. For example, if you want to remember that your office outing is in May, you can visualize the members of your team having a picnic in a field full of flowers. Memorize the list of 12 pegs below, cover them and write out the alphabet backward, then see if you can recall them.

TECHNIQUE: CALENDAR PEG SYSTEM

August

May

July

December

January: Janus, the two-faced god

February: Leaping

March: Marching

April: Apron

May: Flowers

June: Dune

July: Fireworks

August: Vacations

September: Scepter

October: Fall leaves

November: Turkey

December: Presents

TIP

Making your memory cues concrete and visible is a time-honored memory-boosting stratagem. Whether you use a traditional knot in a piece of string or a sticky note on the refrigerator, or whether you can come up with more creative options, mnemonic aides kept in a visible place can help you circumvent memory problems.

6 CALENDAR PEG PRACTICE

Let's try out the calendar peg system—use it to memorize these six important events. When you're done, cover them up, name five ice cream flavors, then see if you can recall them.

1 _____

2 _____

3 _____

4 _____

5 _____

6 _____

6/6: 1 point   Your score _____

February
feed neighbor's cat

March
school party

May
wedding anniversary

September
back to school

October
vacation in France

November
international soccer match

7 DIARY DRAWER

Using the calendar peg system, can you turn these tasks and dates into memorable visual associations? Read the list then sketch simple but striking visual links in your date book. Cover the drawings, then recall the visualizations in order to remember during which month each task or event will take place.

End of season sale: **April**
House insurance renewal: **July**
Car service: **August**
Plant daffodil bulbs: **October**

August

July

October

April

4/4: 1 point   Your score _____

8 BIRTHDAY BIBLE

It's always handy if someone's birthday falls on a memorable date. For example, if Aunt Flora's birthday is on October 31, which is Halloween in many English-speaking countries, you can visualize a Jack O'Lantern, which is symbolic of Halloween, as the face of a flower, to symbolize Flora. By thinking of some striking visuals to help you, practice memorizing these fake relatives' birthdays. Study them for 2 minutes, then cover and answer the questions.

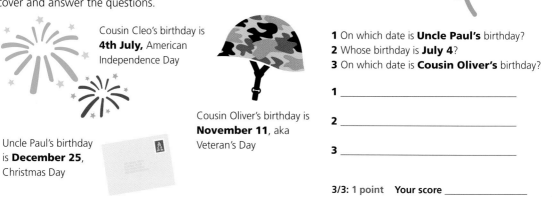

Cousin Cleo's birthday is **4th July,** American Independence Day

Cousin Oliver's birthday is **November 11**, aka Veteran's Day

Uncle Paul's birthday is **December 25**, Christmas Day

1 On which date is **Uncle Paul's** birthday?
2 Whose birthday is **July 4**?
3 On which date is **Cousin Oliver's** birthday?

1 _____

2 _____

3 _____

3/3: 1 point   Your score _____

9 BIRTHDAY BRAINIAC

A more generally applicable system for remembering the day as well as the month is to combine a calendar peg system with a number peg system.

For example, you always forget your niece Belle's birthday is **February 3**.
Your calendar peg for February is a daffodil, so you could visualize Belle holding a daffodil.
Your rhyming number peg for 3 is sea, so you could visualize Belle floating in a boat on the sea.
To combine the two pegs, you could visualize Belle holding a daffodil while floating on a boat on the sea.

Use pegs of your own devising to memorize these birthdays. Then cover them up, recite your phone number backward, and see if you can recall whose birthday is on which date.

Niece Belle: **February 3**
Cousin Willy: **August 13**
Aunt Micha: **March 8**
Cousin Yoko: **April 25**
Nephew Sayed: **November 27**

1 _____

2 _____

3 _____

4 _____

5 _____

5/5: 1 point   Your score _____

10 ANNIVERSARY ACE

Birthdays aren't the only important biographical information you can memorize with a calendar/number peg system combination. Use your personalized system to practice memorizing a few anniversaries of the sort that could really get you trouble if you forget them. Visualize the ones below for 2 minutes, then cover and test your recall after 5 minutes.

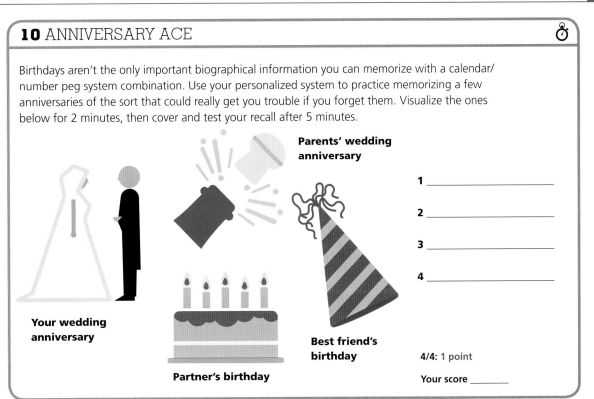

Parents' wedding anniversary

1 _____

2 _____

3 _____

4 _____

Your wedding anniversary

Best friend's birthday

Partner's birthday

4/4: 1 point

Your score _____

11 RETURN DATES

You've borrowed and renewed six books from the library, each due back on a different date. Can you remember the return dates by combining the calendar peg and number peg systems? Memorize, cover, and list eight Asian countries, then write down the due dates.

The Lost World: **January 10**
Around the World in 80 Days: **February 4**
The Hound of the Baskervilles: **April 6**
Treasure Island: **August 1**
Last of the Mohicans: **September 2**
Frankenstein: **November 8**

return by
January 10

1 _____

2 _____

3 _____

4 _____

5 _____

6 _____

6/6: 1 point Your score _____

12 GET KNOTTED

Another type of long-term memory is procedural memory—memory for "how" as opposed to memory for "what." When you learn a skill or routine, from learning to ride a bike to flying an airplane, you are creating long-term procedural memories. A good way to give your procedural memory a workout is to practice a useful or entertaining skill, such as tying a knot. Find two pieces of string or rope, each at least 12in (30cm) long, and follow the simple instructions on the right to make a double fisherman's knot (a useful knot for tying two ropes together). Practice the knot six or seven times, and then come back a day later and try out the knot again. How did you do?

Score 1 point if you tied the knot correctly

Your score _____

1 Lie the ends of the two ropes together.

2 With each rope, make two turns around both ropes, back in the direction of the rest of the rope.

3 Pass the end through the loops and pull each end tight. You should end up with two "x" shapes.

13 KNOT KNOW-HOW

Using your procedural memory not only gives your brain a workout, but also teaches you useful practical skills. For instance, see if you can learn how to tie the knot known as a round turn and two half hitches, useful for tying a rope to a bar or ring. Follow the steps below, practice five or six times, then come back tomorrow and see how many steps you can recall. You can use rope or string.

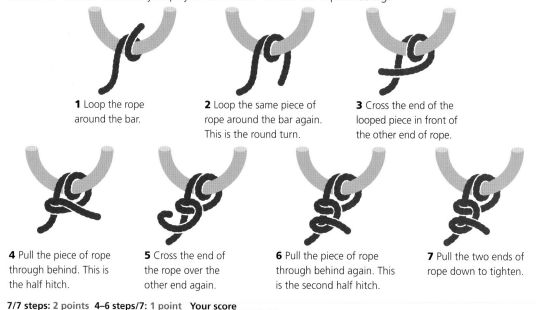

1 Loop the rope around the bar.

2 Loop the same piece of rope around the bar again. This is the round turn.

3 Cross the end of the looped piece in front of the other end of rope.

4 Pull the piece of rope through behind. This is the half hitch.

5 Cross the end of the rope over the other end again.

6 Pull the piece of rope through behind again. This is the second half hitch.

7 Pull the two ends of rope down to tighten.

7/7 steps: 2 points 4–6 steps/7: 1 point   Your score _____

14 PICK UP A PENGUIN

Keep on working your procedural memory by learning to make this origami penguin. Take a square of paper that is colored on one side (this is so the sides are clearly different). Start with the white side down and follow the instructions below. Practice with five squares of paper, then score yourself on how many folds you can remember.

1 Turn the paper and fold in half to make a triangle.

2 Fold a small top edge over. Repeat on the other side.

3 With the sides still folded, open the paper out.

4 Fold a small bottom piece inward.

5 Fold a small top piece behind to form the "head."

6 Fold the paper in half.

7 Push the head upward.

6–7 folds: 2 points
4–5 folds: 1 point

Your score _____

15 ACE OF CUPS

Try this slightly more complex origami challenge—making a simple cup out of paper. Follow the visual instructions below and practice it five times, then score yourself on how many folds you can remember.

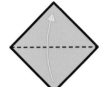 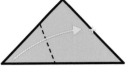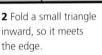

2 Fold a small triangle inward, so it meets the edge.

1 Turn the paper and fold in half to make a triangle.

3 Fold a small triangle on the opposite side, so it aligns with the edge.

4 Fold the first top triangle inward.

5 Fold the second top triangle behind.

6 Pull the top two triangles, so the cup opens.

5–6 folds: 3 points
3–4 folds: 2 points
1–2 folds: 1 point

Your score _____

Your score   **/40**   **30–40 GOLD**

You have an excellent LTM for details big and small. Consider putting your gifts to good use by putting down your biographical memories on paper.

 10–29 SILVER

Your LTM is average. Work through the chapter again in a few days: you may find that your memory has been stimulated in the interval and you can remember more.

 0–9 BRONZE

There are some big spaces in your LTM and you should work on improving your encoding in the future. You can also fill in the blank spaces through exercises that stimulate biographical memories.

 Turn to page 178 for the Challenge

CHAPTER 6

PIN IN A HAYSTACK

PINS AND PASSWORDS

Pin in a haystack

Remembering many passwords and PINs can be tricky, especially as the guidelines governing their creation become ever more constrictive. This chapter will help you to create and recall secure and memorable passwords and provide tips for recalling PINs.

QUESTIONNAIRE
Use this quick quiz to work out whether you're a security nightmare or a password paragon.

1 Can you usually remember all your passwords, or do you have them written down?

Remember/Written down
[score 1 point for "Remember"]

2 Do you frequently get locked out of your bank/email/shopping accounts?

Frequently/Rarely
[score 1 point for "Rarely"]

3 Is your browser set to remember your passwords automatically?

Yes/No
[score 1 point for "No"]

4 Have you left any of your passwords/PINs unchanged from the "password" or "1234" format in which they were initially given to you?

Yes/No [score 1 point for "No"]

5 Have you used your own or a family member's name, your date of birth, a pet's name, or your home address for any of your passwords or PINs?

Yes/No [score 1 point for "No"]

6 Do you have any sort of system for remembering different PINs and passwords, or do you just hope for the best?

System/Hope for the best
[score 1 point for "System"]

How did you score?
0–2: Your memory for PINs and passwords is buckling under the weight of its daily demands, and you're cutting corners and compromising security as a result. The exercises in this chapter should help you devise better and more memorable passwords.

3–4: You struggle to remember all your PINs and passwords, but the tips and techniques in this chapter should help you improve.

5–6: You scored highly, but do you follow good practice on security as well as having a good memory for PINs and passwords? This chapter will help you cover all bases.

1 NAMES AND DATES

A useful source of personal information that combines letters and numbers is birthdays. Try putting together the first few letters of a relative or friend's name with their birth dates (don't use your own). For example, John Smith February 15, 1956, might become JoSm15Feb1956, or maybe 1956Jo15SmFeb. Practice on some of your relatives on a separate piece of paper.

Relative	Name	Birth date
Father	_____	_____
Mother	_____	_____
Grandfather	_____	_____
Grandmother	_____	_____
Sibling	_____	_____

2 LEETSPEAK

Leet derives from a computer user's "elite" status when accessing a software program. Leetspeak became an online alphabet used by cybergeeks, in which the letters of the alphabet are replaced with symbols. This is a good system for creating a secure password. Using this table of leet substitutions, can you encode the five passwords?

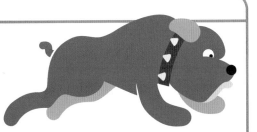

A GOBULLDOGS _____

B XYLOPHONE _____

C BIRTHDAY _____

D CALORIES _____

E WHITEHOUSE _____

A @	B |3	C (	D |)	E 3	F |=
G 9	H #	I !	J _|	K 1<	L 1
M IVI	N I\I	O *	P IO	Q O_	R |2
S $	T 7	U L|	V V	W VV	X %
Y '/,	Z 2				

Answers on page 180

5/5: 1 point **Your score** _____

TIP

If you need help remembering a password, do not write down the password itself. Write a prompt or question, based on something personal, which will make sense to you but not to a thief. For example, if your password is based on something to do with a relative, use a private family nickname to remind you of the identity of the person.

3 STACKED UP

A clever trick that transforms your keyboard into a code machine is to use the column of letters under each number. For example, on the keyboard below, letters Q, A, and Z are below the number 1 key, while below the 6 are Y, H, and N (keyboards can differ so make sure you base your system on one that you use all the time). You can use this as the basis for a secure password by remembering a short number sequence, such as an important year, and typing all the letters under each number. For example, using the keyboard below, 1980 would be qazol.ik,p;/ Practice on these numbers.

Numbers	Password
A 4046	_____
B 1979	_____
C 2005	_____
D 8238	_____

Answers on page 180
Score 4/4: 1 point   Your score _____

4 BASE SYSTEM

Your passwords may be individually memorable, but how can you remember which one goes with which website or account? One way of doing so is to create a secure base password that you can use across multiple sites. Your base password is then individually tailored to each website or account, so you don't run the security risk of using the same password multiple times. The aim of this system is that you have to remember only your base password. The sites themselves then supply the key extra piece of information.

For your base password, make an acronym of something memorable, such as your favorite book, film title, or a line from a poem. For example, the phrase "Four And Twenty Blackbirds Baked In A Pie" becomes "4A20BBIAP". Practice creating a base password on the following:

A All For One And One For All   _____

B I Am 16 Going On 17   _____

C Three Blind Mice, See How They Run   _____

D Around The World In 80 Days   _____

Answers on page 180
Score 4/4: 1 point   Your score _____

5 SYSTEM ADDICT

If your base password does not contain any numbers, then it is a good idea to incorporate some. This will make your base much more secure. One easy and memorable way to do this is to precede the password with the number of words in the acronym. For example *Tyger, Tyger, Burning Bright, In The Forests Of The Night* becomes 10TTBBITFOTN. Practice creating memorable but secure base passwords with these examples.

Full length   **Base password**

A The Unbearable Lightness Of Being   _____

B You Can't Always Get What You Want   _____

C To Kill A Mockingbird   _____

D Red Sky At Night, Sailor's Delight   _____

Answers on page 181

4/4: 1 point Your score _____

6 BESPOKE PASSWORDS

Now practice modifying your base password to link it to the website for which it is used. A simple way to tailor the base password is to add three letters or numbers to it from the site or account name. For example, if your base password is 10TTBBITFOTN and the site is called www.moneybank.com, your site specific password could become mon10TTBBITFOTN. Using the same base, create passwords for these example sites:

Site   **Bespoke password**

A www.green.com   _____

B www.evensquare.com   _____

C www.y3ksounds.org   _____

D www.legalbet.com   _____

Answers on page 181

Score 4/4: 1 point Your score _____

7 CONSONANT SWAP

Another way to tailor your base password to each site is to substitute letters from the site name into your base, according to a preset rule. For example, you might have a rule that says "swap vowels in the site name with consonants in your base (as far as the number of letters will allow)." So for the website www.oakdoor.com and the base 10TTBBITFOTN you would swap the O for T, A for T, O for B, and O for B. Your password would become 10OAOOITFOTN. Practice using this rule with the same base and the example sites:

Site	Bespoke password
A www.green.co.uk	_____
B www.evensquare.com	_____
C www.y3ksounds.org	_____
D www.legalbet.com	_____

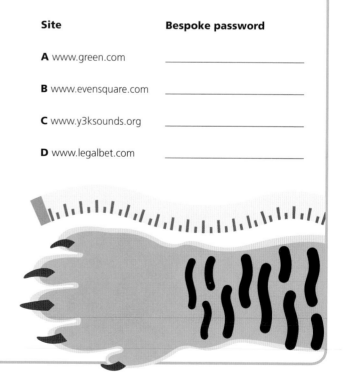

Answers on page 181

Score 4/4: **1 point** **Your score** _____

8 MADE TO MEASURE

You can make your base password even more secure and still tailor it to a website by changing it according to a characteristic of the site name. For instance, as well as adding the first letters of the site name you could also change the length of the base, so your password has an equal number of letters from both the website and the base. For example, suppose your base password is 10TTBBITFOTN, and the website is oakdoor. You could take the first 4 letters of oakdoor and match it with the first 4 characters of your base to get the password oakd10TT. Using the same base, tailor passwords for the same example sites:

Site	Bespoke password
A www.green.com	_____
B www.evensquare.com	_____
C www.y3ksounds.org	_____
D www.legalbet.com	_____

Answers on page 181

Score 4/4: **1 point** **Your score** _____

9 PASSWORD CREATION

Using your preferred system(s) from the password exercises you've just completed, create your own secure passwords for each of the eight vacation-related websites below. Try to remember these passwords because you will be tested on them later in the chapter.

www.bank.com _____

www.willneedcar.com _____

www.bookonbeach.com _____

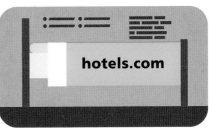

www.somewheretostay.com _____

www.moreclothes.com _____

www.bookwithus.com _____

www.flycheaply.com _____

www.mustbuyinsurance.com _____

10 PIN PRACTICE

Personal Identification Numbers (PINs) are only four digits long, but hard to remember when you have half a dozen of them jostling for space in your head. To set a baseline for your ability to remember PINs, try committing these four to memory, then cover them and come back at least an hour later to test your recall.

6012 _____

5585 _____

1003 _____

9174 _____

Score 4/4: 1 point   Your score _____

11 UP STACKED

The number stack system (see page 86) works in reverse to help you remember PINs. Each number in a four-digit PIN gives at least one corresponding letter option. Use these to then make a word or memorable acrostic. For example, if your PIN is 6546, you could choose the letters H, T, F, and N to come up with the acrostic Hard To Forget Now. If you have access to a keyboard, all you have to do is remember the acrostic. Using the keyboard below, work out these PINs from their acrostics, within 1 minute.

Acrostic   **PIN**

A Too Easy To Remember   _____

B I Love Purple Shoes   _____

C North South East West   _____

D Once Upon A Time   _____

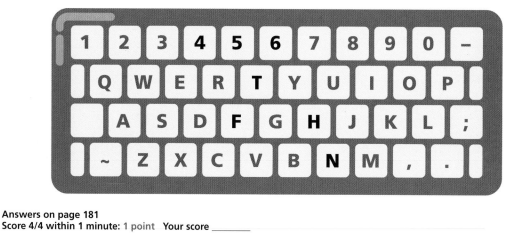

Answers on page 181
Score 4/4 within 1 minute: 1 point   Your score _____

12 FOUR-WORD DECODER

Linking your PIN to a visual sentence is a good way of recalling the numbers. Use the numbers in a PIN to dictate the length of the words in a four-word sentence. For example, 3734 would yield a sentence with words three letters, seven letters, three letters, and four letters long respectively. For example, "bad manners are rude". Based on the number of letters in the words in the phrases below, can you decode them into PINs? Cover the PINs, wait 30 minutes, and see if you can write them down on a separate piece of paper.

Four-word sentence	PIN
Dancing down the road	_____
Happy hippos gamble gladly	_____
Little ants attacked me	_____
Men wearing enormous pants	_____
Into the unknown outside	_____

Score 5/5: **1 point** Your score _____

13 FOUR-WORD KEYS

Now practice generating your own four-word sentences. For each of the three PINs below, can you devise a four-word mnemonic? When you have done so, come back to the exercise after an hour and, with the PINs and mnemonics covered up, see if you can recall the PINs using your mnemonics, on a separate piece of paper.

PIN	Four-word sentence
5324	_____
	_____
8437	_____
	_____
6244	_____
	_____

Score 3/3: **1 point** Your score _____

TIP

Some of the more realistic cyber-security experts concede that if it's a choice between people using unsafe passwords or writing something down, the latter may be more secure. With a secret note you can physically control access to it as well as physically concealing it, and you are more likely to be able to tell if security has been compromised. So consider writing down at least a cryptic hint for self-reminder purposes.

14 LETTER PAIRS

A simple mnemonic technique for PINs is to treat the numbers as code for a sequence of letters. Let the first 10 letters of the alphabet correspond to the numbers 0–9 and translate your PIN into a four-letter sequence: A would be 0, B would be 1 and so on. If you treat these four numbers as two pairs of letters and use the pairs as the initials of famous people, you have a base for a memorable visualization. For example, if your PIN is 1631, the corresponding letter pairs will be B (1) G (6) and D (3) B (1), which could suggest the famous names Bee Gees and David Beckham. Come up with a visualization to combine the two names and you have a mnemonic for your PIN. Try the technique on these PINs, using a separate piece of paper if necessary.

PIN	Letters	Famous names	Visualization
4407	_____	_____	_____
6383	_____	_____	_____
3251	_____	_____	_____

15 LETTER PAIRS PLUS

Using only the first 10 letters of the alphabet is restrictive. To use the full range for the same initials-generating technique, refer to a table like this:

0	1	2	3	4	5	6	7	8	9
A	B	C	D	E	F	G	H	I	J
K	L	M	N	O	P	Q	R	S	T
U	V	W	X	Y	Z				

Use the table to work out the PINs represented by these famous pairs. Then cover the PINs and table and try to recall the PINs 5 minutes later.

Names	Initials	Corresponding PIN
A Arnold Schwarzenegger and The Pink Panther	_____	_____
B Tom Cruise and John Travolta	_____	_____
C Woody Allen and Barack Obama	_____	_____
D Elvis Presley and Mahatma Gandhi	_____	_____

Answers on page 181
Score 4/4: 1 point   Your score _____

16 WORD PINS

For some PINs, the number–letter system will yield letter sequences that are words or are close to words: for example, 5748 converts to PRES, which is short for "president." In such cases you will only need to remember a single word. Using the chart of number–letter correspondences in Exercise 15, turn these PINs into words, commit them to memory, and then cover the list. Write down eight American actors, and see if you can remember the words and the numbers to which they correspond.

PIN	Word	PIN recall
8203	_____	_____
3429	_____	_____
1011	_____	_____
0836	_____	_____
4668	_____	_____

5/5: 3 points 4/5: 2 points 3/5: 1 point Your score ____

17 PIN PUNS

Some numbers have obvious associations; for example, 4 is the number of sides in a square. Use common associations like this as the basis for creating memorable visualizations, and if possible make them humorous. For example, 3375 might suggest two triangles (3 being the number of sides of a triangle) and a grandfather (75 could be the age of your grandfather when you were born). This could suggest the image of a grandfather trying to ride a bicycle with two triangular wheels. Come up with memorable visuals for these PINs, then try to recall them after 30 minutes.

PIN	Visualization
7213	_____
	_____
9249	_____
	_____
1001	_____
	_____
1865	_____
	_____

4/4: 1 point Your score _____

18 NUMBER RHYMES

You can use rhymes to help remember your PINs. Write down memorable rhyming words for numbers 0–9. Once you've come up with a list of rhyming words, use them to create a sentence with a memorable visualization for your PINs. For example, if your PIN was 8513, you could create the visual sentence: a great (8) drive (5) in the sun (1) to a tree (3). See if you can use your rhyming words to think of visualizations for the following PINs. Now cover the PINs and after 30 minutes see if you can recall the PINs through the visualizations.

6036

	Visualization	**PIN recall**
6036	_____	_____
1523	_____	_____
8470	_____	_____
9845	_____	_____

Score **1 point** for each PIN you remember   Your score _____

19 THIS OLD MAN

Another system for turning numbers into memorable images is based on nursery rhymes, such as *This Old Man,* which rhymes numbers with words. For example, two and shoe, three and knee. You can then use these words to construct a visualization. On the right are the rhymes from *This Old Man*, plus an extra one for zero.

Using the rhymes for *This Old Man*, can you decode these sentences into their corresponding PINs?

A Use shoes and thumbs to push open the gate to heaven   **PIN** _____

B Superhero uses a stick to open door to reveal a beehive   **PIN** _____

C Shoes that are best for your spine and knees are by the door   **PIN** _____

Number	Rhyme
one	thumb
two	shoe
three	knee
four	door
five	hive
six	sticks
seven	heaven
eight	gate
nine	spine
zero	hero

20 PASSWORD RECALL

Your week of sun and sand—all booked and arranged online—turns into an eventful trip. At an internet café, you need to access the various sites you used to arrange the holiday, but can you remember all the passwords you created on page 89?

You want to book another excursion through the same company. Recall your password to book again.

www.bookwithus.com

_____

It's time to check in for the flight home. What is your password for the airline website?

www.flycheaply.com

_____

The hotel cannot find your booking. Log on to your account to find the booking confirmation.

www.somewheretostay.com

_____

You've finished all your books. Can you access the online bookstore to download more?

www.bookonbeach.com

_____

You need to make a claim on your travel insurance. Log on to your account to find your policy.

www.mustbuyinsurance.com

_____

Your wallet has been stolen. Can you recall your password for your bank to transfer emergency funds?

www.bank.com

_____

You've been given a small car, when you booked a large family car. Log on to the car rental website to sort it out.

www.willneedcarhire.com

_____

The online department store sent you the wrong clothing items. Log on to the site to request a return.

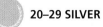

www.moreclothes.com

_____

Score 1 point for each password you remembered   **Your score** _____

Your score   **/35**   **30–35 GOLD**

Your memory for passwords and PINs is impressive—keep practicing your memorization techniques to make them perfect.

20–29 SILVER

Your memory for passwords and PINs is fair, but could improve. Revisit the methods of memorization in this chapter and keep practicing them.

0–19 BRONZE

PINs and passwords pose a significant challenge to your memory abilities. Go back and work through the chapter again.

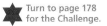

Turn to page 178 for the Challenge.

CHAPTER 7
REVISION EXPRESS
RECALL OF FACTS

Revision express

Any memory that can be recalled after a minute has been stored in your long-term memory. A subcategory of long-term memory is semantic memory, which is knowledge-based and not related to personal, or emotional, experiences. Facts, rules, meanings and any general knowledge you have learned are all stored, and retrieved, from your semantic memory.

QUESTIONNAIRE

Are you a quiz champion and exam expert or a forgetful fumbler of facts? Use this quick quiz to see how your semantic memory shapes up in your everyday life.

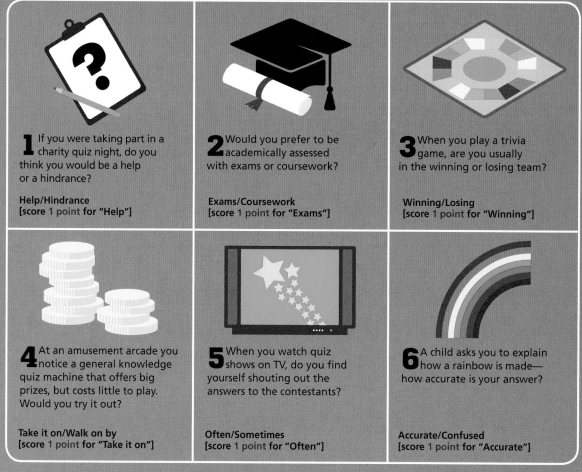

1 If you were taking part in a charity quiz night, do you think you would be a help or a hindrance?

Help/Hindrance
[score 1 point for "Help"]

2 Would you prefer to be academically assessed with exams or coursework?

Exams/Coursework
[score 1 point for "Exams"]

3 When you play a trivia game, are you usually in the winning or losing team?

Winning/Losing
[score 1 point for "Winning"]

4 At an amusement arcade you notice a general knowledge quiz machine that offers big prizes, but costs little to play. Would you try it out?

Take it on/Walk on by
[score 1 point for "Take it on"]

5 When you watch quiz shows on TV, do you find yourself shouting out the answers to the contestants?

Often/Sometimes
[score 1 point for "Often"]

6 A child asks you to explain how a rainbow is made—how accurate is your answer?

Accurate/Confused
[score 1 point for "Accurate"]

How did you score?

0–2: Your knowledge base is lacking—you probably need to work on boosting both your encoding and retrieval of semantic memory.

3–4: Your semantic memory is average. The exercises and challenges in this chapter should help you to reach the top of the class.

5–6: You're a bit of a boffin, but you can always do better. The exercises in this chapter should help hone your mental edge.

1 QUIZ MASTER

A good way to get a baseline of your semantic memory is to test your general knowledge. See how you score in this test.

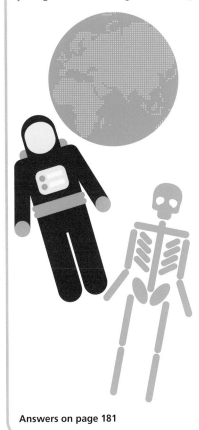

1 What is the second most populous nation on Earth?

2 Who composed the Moonlight Sonata?

3 Can you name all the world's oceans?

4 Complete Sir Isaac Newton's famous third law of motion: "For every action..."

5 In which country was the compass invented?

6 What year was the Russian Revolution?

7 Who was the second man on the Moon?

8 What is the longest bone in the body?

9 Which national team won the first football World Cup?

10 Which individual has won the most Oscars?

1 _____

2 _____

3 _____

4 _____

5 _____

6 _____

7 _____

8 _____

9 _____

10 _____

Score 1 point for each correct answer

Your score _____

Answers on page 181

2 SPOT THE LINK

There are more (and arguably better) ways to test knowledge than a straightforward general knowledge quiz. For instance, putting your knowledge to work in a test such as this: can you work out what these countries have in common?

Luxembourg

San Marino

Bolivia

Nepal

Paraguay

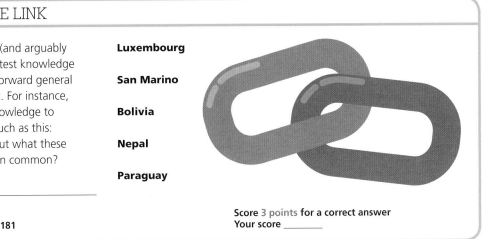

Answer_____

Answer on page 181

Score 3 points for a correct answer
Your score _____

TECHNIQUE: MNEMONIC ACROSTIC

A mnemonic is a device that aids memorization. An acrostic is one example of a mnemonic. Here, a list of facts to be memorized is replaced with a more memorable list of words with the same initial letter. Acrostics can be very helpful when you need to remember facts in a particular order. Here is an example of an acrostic to help you remember the order of the planets from the Sun. When prompted, your acrostic should spring to mind, and can then be converted back into the fact.

Fact	**Acrostic**	**Prompt**
Order of the planets from the Sun (Mercury, Venus, Earth, Mars, Jupiter, Saturn, Uranus, Neptune)	My Very Easy Method: Just Sit Up Nights	Name the planets in order

3 MORE MNEMONIC ACROSTICS

Try out some more acrostics for a rapid-learning technique. See if you can devise memorable acrostics to help you recall these three facts, then give yourself 30 seconds to learn them. Cover and use the prompt to test your recall after waiting 5 minutes.

Fact	**Acrostic**	**Prompt**	**Fact recall**
Attributes of living things in biology (Nutrition, Irritability, Movement, Growth, Respiration, Reproduction, Excretion)	_____ _____	List the attributes of living things in biology	_____ _____
Order in which notes fall on the treble clef (EGBDF)	_____ _____	List the notes of the treble clef in order	_____
How to spell "rhythm"	_____ _____	Spell the word that means the regular beat of a piece of music	_____

3/3: 1 point Your score _____

100

TECHNIQUE: BACKGROUND CHECK

Mnemonics can help you to commit small pieces of information to memory, but a large amount of information needs a more comprehensive solution. The first step in boosting memory for semantic knowledge is to improve encoding – facts become more memorable when they are learned in context, rather than in isolation. In other words, learning additional information can make the central data easier to remember.

On the right is an isolated fact, then a different fact accompanied by some background information. Read both, then wait 20 minutes before returning and testing for recall (with the information covered up). It should be easier to remember the fact with extra information.

Isolated fact
Chemical symbol for silver: Ag

Fact with background information
Chemical symbol for sodium: Na.
Na derives from natron, the Egyptian word for salt, because sodium is one of the elements that makes up salt (sodium chloride).
The Egyptians used natron to dry out and preserve corpses as part of the mummification process.

4 BACKGROUND CHECK PRACTICE

Read the following facts and concentrate carefully on their background information to help you encode them. Now cover the facts and the background information, wait 5 minutes, then see if you can answer the questions below.

The newton is the unit for force
The unit for force is named after physicist Sir Issac Newton, whose third law of motion stated that for every force acting in one direction, there is an equal force acting in the opposite direction.

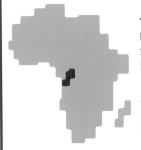

The capital of the Republic of Congo is Brazzaville
Brazzaville is named after the Italian-French explorer Pierre Savorgnan de Brazza. Brazza's explorations along the Congo River helped France establish its colony known as French Congo.

Antonin Dvořák was a Czech composer
Dvořák was born in Bohemia, then part of the Austro-Hungarian Empire. He studied at the Organ School in Prague.

Quiz questions

1 What is the capital of the Republic of Congo? _____

2 What is the unit for force? _____

3 What nationality was Dvořák? _____

Score 1 point **for each correct answer**   Your score _____

TECHNIQUE: TOPLINE

One of the keys to better revision is smarter revision. Don't try to commit whole chunks of text to memory; work through the text and identify the topline facts and key words—these can become the bullet points that you should try to commit to memory. For example, on the right is a small extract about bats from an encyclopedia of animals.

You could pick out the following bullet points from it:

• **Bats are the only mammals that can fly, rather than glide.**
• **The wing membrane is called the patagium.**

Bats are the only mammals that possess true, flapping wings and the ability to fly (as opposed to colugos, for example, which glide). Bats' wing membrane (the patagium), an extension of the skin of the back and belly, provides a high degree of maneuverability in flight.

5 TOPLINE PRACTICE

Here is the rest of the passage on bats from the encyclopedia. Can you highlight five topline facts within the passage, then recall them below after 30 minutes.

1 _____
_____

2 _____
_____

3 _____
_____

4 _____
_____

5 _____
_____

How many facts did you recall?
5/5: score 2 points
3–4/5: score 1 point

Your score _____

Bats' wingspans range from over 5ft (1.5m) in the large flying fox to as little as 6in (15cm) in the hog-nosed bat. More than half the species echolocate to capture prey and to navigate at night. Chiroptera is a huge order that comprises nearly a quarter of all mammal species and is exceeded only by rodents in terms of species numbers. Bats are common in tropical and temperate habitats worldwide, but are not found in environments that are too cold to support a source of food, such as the polar regions. When used in flight, echolocation makes bats formidable hunters. Sounds ("clicks") are produced in the larynx, emitted through the nose or mouth, and directed or focused by the nose leaf (if present). Once the clicks have reflected off an object, the returning echo is picked up via the bat's sensitive ears. The time it takes to receive the echo reveals the size and location of anything in the bat's path.

A popular visual tool for boosting learning and revision, which can help with both encoding and retrieval, is a Mind Web. This is a diagram showing information, or just single words, in boxes or circles, and associated words or concepts joined to them and to other information by lines, to give a branching, treelike structure radiating out from the center. The addition of graphics adds a visual element to the Mind Web, which can aid semantic memorization. Below is a simple example based around a play you might be studying. Can you draw a Mind Web for a topic of your choice?

TECHNIQUE: MENTAL MAPPING

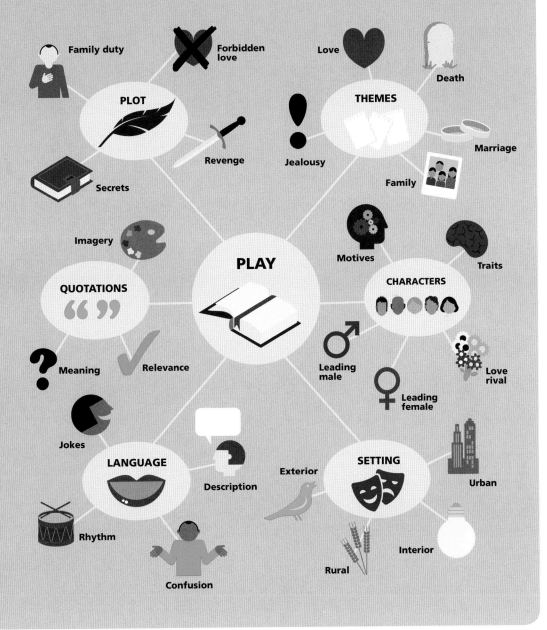

Family duty · Forbidden love · Love · Death · PLOT · THEMES · Revenge · Jealousy · Marriage · Secrets · Family · Imagery · Motives · Traits · PLAY · QUOTATIONS · CHARACTERS · Meaning · Relevance · Leading male · Love rival · Leading female · Jokes · Description · Exterior · Urban · LANGUAGE · SETTING · Rhythm · Interior · Confusion · Rural

Visualization can help you learn and remember all sorts of facts. For instance, if you are 6ft (1.8m) tall, you could remember that the longest boa constrictor ever found was 18ft (5.4m) long, by picturing three of you alongside it end to end. Try to think of a visualization for the facts you need to learn and see if you find them easier to recall.

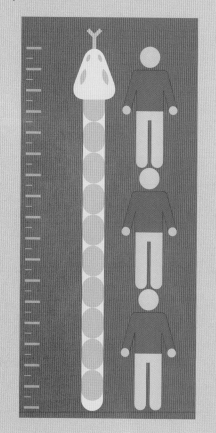

6 SCIENCE FICTION PRACTICE

Practice some visual associations on these science facts, then see if you can answer the questions 10 minutes later.

Nitrogen is the most common gas in the atmosphere.

The dinosaurs died out **65 million years ago**.

The nearest star to our Solar System is **Proxima Centauri**.

Almost 50 percent of a human being's DNA is identical to that of a **banana**.

Rivers and lakes account for less than **0.007 percent** of the Earth's water.

_____ is the most common gas in the atmosphere.

The dinosaurs died out _____

The nearest star to our Solar System is _____

What percentage of DNA do humans share with a banana? _____

Rivers and lakes account for less than _____ percent of the Earth's water.

Score 1 point for each fact you remembered.

Your score _____

Repeating an act of memorization five times is believed to fix a fact irrevocably in your LTM. Whether or not this is true, it certainly helps to review pieces of information at regular intervals—frequently at first, then at longer intervals. For instance, review first after an hour, then after a day, then after a week.

Peg systems involve learning a memorable series, which can then form the basis of a sequence of visualizations (see pages 50, 62, and 76 for examples). The body makes a good basis for a peg system, if you learn its "numbering." Learn all the locations and you can memorize lists up to 15 items long—more if you wish to create further pegs. For example, if you needed to memorize the instruments in an orchestra, you could relate the first instrument on your list, for example a violin, to the first body peg, in this example the head. So you could visualize the violin's resonances (the f-shaped airholes) as a mustache. Study the list of pegs below for as long as you need, then cover it and write down all the locations in order.

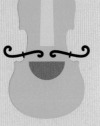

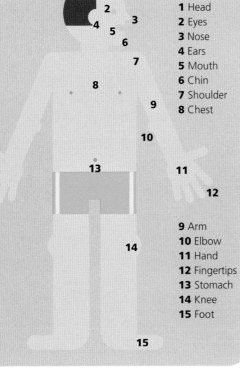

1 Head
2 Eyes
3 Nose
4 Ears
5 Mouth
6 Chin
7 Shoulder
8 Chest
9 Arm
10 Elbow
11 Hand
12 Fingertips
13 Stomach
14 Knee
15 Foot

TECHNIQUE: BODY PEG SYSTEM

7 BATTLE STATIONS

Try out the body peg system by learning this list of major battles of World War Two. Link the first battle on the list to the first peg of the human body and form a visualization for each battle. Cover the list, name five species of trees, and see if you can reproduce it.

1 Battle of Dunkirk
2 Battle of the River Plate
3 Battle of Britain
4 Attack on Pearl Harbor
5 The Battle of Moscow
6 The Battle of Stalingrad
7 The Fall of Singapore
8 D-Day Landings
9 The Battle of Arnhem
10 The Battle of the Bulge
11 The Battle of Berlin
12 The Battle of Coral Sea
13 The Battle of Midway
14 The Battle of Guadalcanal
15 The Battle of the Philippine Sea

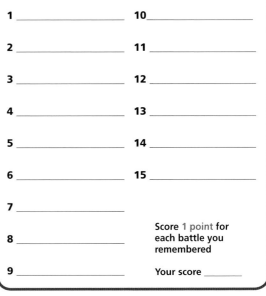

1 _____ 10 _____
2 _____ 11 _____
3 _____ 12 _____
4 _____ 13 _____
5 _____ 14 _____
6 _____ 15 _____
7 _____
8 _____ **Score 1 point for each battle you remembered**
9 _____ **Your score** _____

8 FACTUAL STORIES

Another peg system that can work well for semantic knowledge is taking a familiar narrative and using the narrative's stages as pegs. You can then create visualizations between your list of facts to remember and the pegs. For instance, take the tale of The Hare and the Tortoise. You could peg events from Australian history to the stages of the story. Use the information below as the basis for a series of visualizations, then cover the first column and test for recall in 10 minutes.

Australian history	Hare & Tortoise
First humans cross from Indonesia	Hare laughs at slow Tortoise
Evolution of Aboriginal culture	Tortoise challenges Hare
Introduction of dingo	Hare takes early lead
First European explorers sight Australia	Hare takes nap
Captain Cook visits Australia	Tortoise overtakes Hare
Establishment of Sydney colony	Hare wakes up
Circumnavigation of Australia	Tortoise wins race

Score **1 point** for each event you remembered and **2 extra points** if they are in the correct order   Your score _____

1 _____

2 _____

3 _____

4 _____

5 _____

6 _____

7 _____

9 OPERATIC PROGRESS

Another type of peg system, related to the one above, is the journey system (see page 62), in which stages in a memorable journey are the pegs, and the items to remember are connected to those journey stages through visualizations. Can you commit to memory seven operas by Mozart using stages on a familiar journey such as your commute to work? Use the system to memorize them, then cover the list, write down the names of five rivers, and see if you can remember the operas in order.

Don Giovanni
Così fan tutte
The Impresario
The Magic Flute
The Shepherd King
The Marriage of Figaro
Thamos, King of Egypt

1 _____

2 _____

3 _____

4 _____

5 _____

6 _____

7 _____

Score **1 point** for each opera you remembered   Your score _____

10 POET'S CORNER

Use one of the techniques described in this chapter to memorize the list of famous 19th-century poets below. Once you've committed the list to memory, cover it up, wait 10 minutes, then see if you can name all the poets on the list.

Emily Dickinson
Thomas Hardy
Walt Whitman
Wilfred Owen
Robert William Service
Harriet Beecher Stowe
Robert Graves

1 _____   6 _____

2 _____   7 _____

3 _____

4 _____   Score **1 point** for each
                     poet you remembered

5 _____   **Your score** _____

11 MOBS AND GANGS

Now choose a different technique from the chapter and practice using it to memorize this list of collective nouns for animals. Once you've committed the list to memory, cover it up, list your five favorite books, and see if you can remember all the collective nouns.

A gang of elks   **A parliament of rooks**
A murder of crows   **An unkindness of ravens**
                           A labor of moles
                           A pod of porpoises
                           A mob of kangaroos

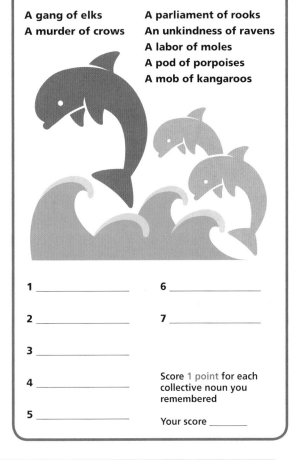

1 _____   6 _____

2 _____   7 _____

3 _____

4 _____   Score **1 point** for each
                     collective noun you
                     remembered

5 _____   **Your score** _____

Your score   **/75**   **60–75 GOLD**

You are a trivia sponge and excellent at learning new information. The tips and techniques in this chapter may help you become even more effective.

30–59 SILVER

You find some topic areas tougher than others, and possibly some techniques more effective than others. Identify which techniques work best for you and stick to those.

0–29 BRONZE

You are struggling to learn/remember new facts. Have another look at the techniques in this chapter: they might help improve your ability to encode and retrieve, preparing you for another assault on the exercises.

Turn to page 179 for the Challenge.

CHAPTER 8

A HEAD FOR FIGURES

BASIC NUMERACY

A head for figures

This chapter looks at the simplest forms of numerical intelligence, from basic arithmetic and proportions to "real world" problems involving simple math. Where possible, do the calculations in your head and use a calculator only where indicated.

QUESTIONNAIRE
Are you a human calculator or a calculating catastrophe? Take this quick quiz to see how your math skills match up.

1 When you buy a couple of items at the local store, do you get the exact change ready or do you wait for the cashier to tell you what the total is?

Change/Wait
[score 1 point for "Change"]

2 You and three friends are splitting the check at a restaurant. Do you work out what everyone owes or pass the check to someone else?

You/Someone else
[score 1 point for "You"]

3 At the deli counter the olives are priced by weight, and the store assistant tells you how much a full container weighs. Can you work out what it will cost?

Easily/Not a chance
[score 1 point for "Easily"]

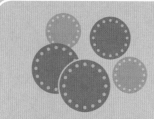

4 You weight is in pounds and ounces, but the doctor wants it in kilograms. Given the conversion factor, would you find it easy or tough to work out the conversion without a calculator?

Easy/Tough
[score 1 point for "Easy"]

5 If you have to add up five or more single-digit numbers, do you work it out in your head or on paper?

Head/Paper [score 1 point for "Head"]

6 There are only three donuts left in the box, but four of you crave something sweet and tasty. Can you figure out how to divide the three donuts fairly?

Yes/No [score 1 point for "Yes"]

How did you score?
0–2: Basic numeracy is a problem, which can be frustrating in day-to-day life and could have serious consequences in areas such as personal finance and financial security. Working through this chapter will give your arithmetic skills a workout and should boost your confidence.

3–4: Your basic numerical reasoning skills are average, but there is plenty of room for improvement by giving your brain an arithmetical workout.
5–6: You are numerate, but how speedy are you when it comes to mental arithmetic? Hone your skills by seeing how fast you can blitz through these exercises.

1 ARITHMETIC 101

Calculating in your head, can you do these problems?

A 337 + 884 = _____

B 7,206 + 5,997 = _____

C 543 – 297 = _____

D 11,063 – 7,789 = _____

E 63 x 11 = _____

F 76 x 87 = _____

G 121 ÷ 11 = _____

H 91 ÷ 7 = _____

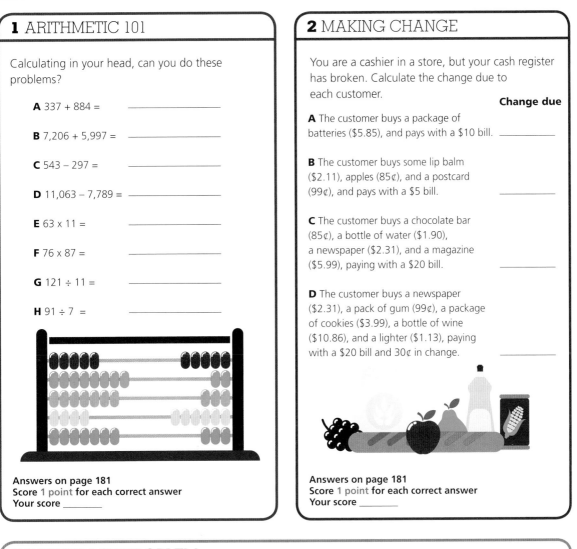

Answers on page 181
Score 1 point for each correct answer
Your score _____

2 MAKING CHANGE

You are a cashier in a store, but your cash register has broken. Calculate the change due to each customer.

Change due

A The customer buys a package of batteries ($5.85), and pays with a $10 bill. _____

B The customer buys some lip balm ($2.11), apples (85¢), and a postcard (99¢), and pays with a $5 bill. _____

C The customer buys a chocolate bar (85¢), a bottle of water ($1.90), a newspaper ($2.31), and a magazine ($5.99), paying with a $20 bill. _____

D The customer buys a newspaper ($2.31), a pack of gum (99¢), a package of cookies ($3.99), a bottle of wine ($10.86), and a lighter ($1.13), paying with a $20 bill and 30¢ in change. _____

Answers on page 181
Score 1 point for each correct answer
Your score _____

3 PAPERBACK PROBLEM

At the bookstore you find three books you want to buy. You only have $17.50—which books can you afford and how much change you will receive?

The Secret Lives of Aunts

$7.99

$9.99

Coffee and Cheese

Year of the Yak

$8.99

Answer _____

Answer on page 181
Score 1 point for a correct answer **Your score** _____

4 CANDY CONUNDRUM

There are five jars of candy behind the counter at the candy shop, labeled with the price for one of each. You have 95¢ to spend. What is the maximum number you can get for your money?

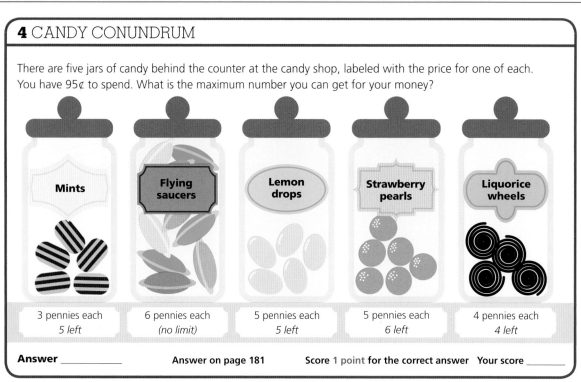

Mints	Flying saucers	Lemon drops	Strawberry pearls	Liquorice wheels
3 pennies each	6 pennies each	5 pennies each	5 pennies each	4 pennies each
5 left	*(no limit)*	*5 left*	*6 left*	*4 left*

Answer _____   Answer on page 181   Score **1 point** for the correct answer   Your score _____

5 ARE YOU COORDINATED?

Graphs are a way of mapping points and lines according to their coordinates in a two-dimensional space. If X is the horizontal axis and Y is the vertical axis, what are the coordinates of the points on this graph? Give the x axis coordinate first.

A _____

B _____

C _____

D _____

E _____

Answers on page 181
5/5: **1 point** Your score _____

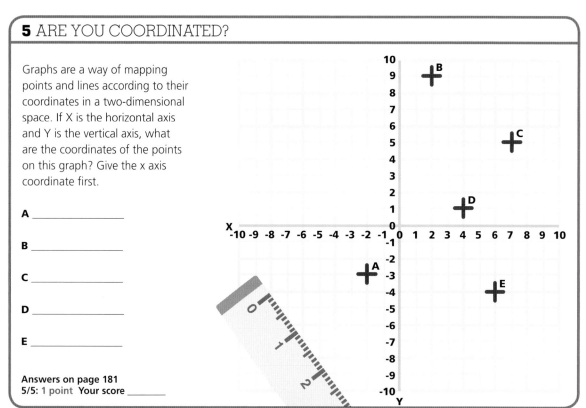

6 GOLDEN BOOTY

The king has two chests in his treasure chamber—a wooden chest and a heavy-lidded steel chest. He moves a bag of 100 gold coins from the wooden chest to the steel chest. He now has three times as many coins in the steel chest as he has in the wooden one. He has 2,000 coins in total. How many coins were in each chest before he moved the bag?

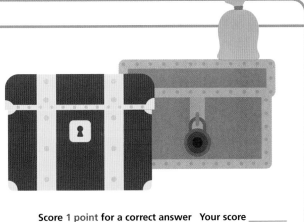

Answer _____   **Answer on page 181**   Score **1 point** for a correct answer   **Your score** _____

7 WHICH IS BIGGER? I

Rank these fractions in order of size, from the biggest to the smallest:

$\frac{3}{4}$ **1** _____

$\frac{2}{3}$ **2** _____

$\frac{7}{8}$ **3** _____

$\frac{9}{16}$ **4** _____

$\frac{2}{5}$ **5** _____

$\frac{5}{15}$ **6** _____

Answer on page 181
6/6: 1 point   Your score _____

8 WHICH IS BIGGER? II

Rank these fractions in order of size, from the biggest to the smallest:

$\frac{5}{8}$

$\frac{15}{32}$

$\frac{2}{3}$

$\frac{6}{10}$

$\frac{9}{12}$

$\frac{8}{15}$

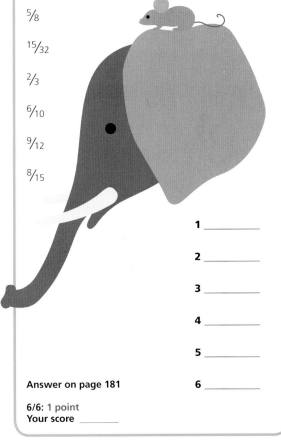

1 _____

2 _____

3 _____

4 _____

5 _____

Answer on page 181   **6** _____

6/6: 1 point
Your score _____

9 DECIMALS VS FRACTIONS I

Rank these fractions and decimals in order of size, from the biggest to the smallest:

0.6   0.3

²⁄₃   0.8

¼   ²⁄₆

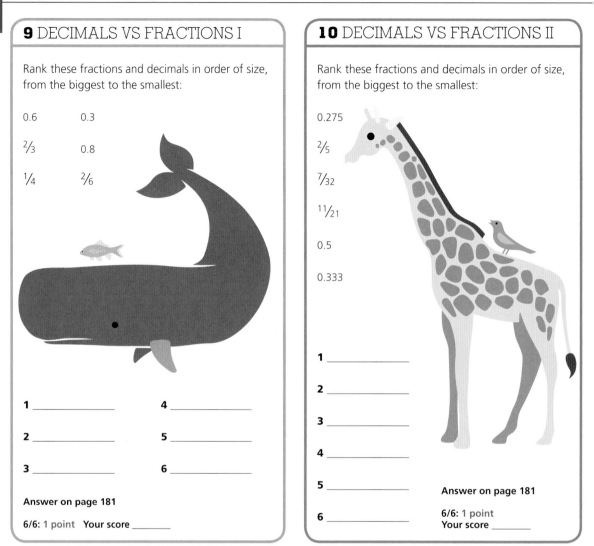

1 _____   4 _____

2 _____   5 _____

3 _____   6 _____

Answer on page 181

6/6: 1 point   Your score _____

10 DECIMALS VS FRACTIONS II

Rank these fractions and decimals in order of size, from the biggest to the smallest:

0.275

²⁄₅

⁷⁄₃₂

¹¹⁄₂₁

0.5

0.333

1 _____

2 _____

3 _____

4 _____

5 _____

6 _____

Answer on page 181

6/6: 1 point
Your score _____

11 SOCK PUZZLE

Derek has checked socks and spotted socks. For every six pairs of checked socks he buys nine pairs of spotted socks. If there are 50 pairs of socks in his sock drawer, how many pairs of checked socks does he have?

Answer _____

Answer on page 182   Score 1 point for a correct answer   Your score _____

12 SLICE OF THE PIE

A pie chart is a graphical representation of proportions. Can you write as a fraction, the proportions represented by each slice of these pie charts?

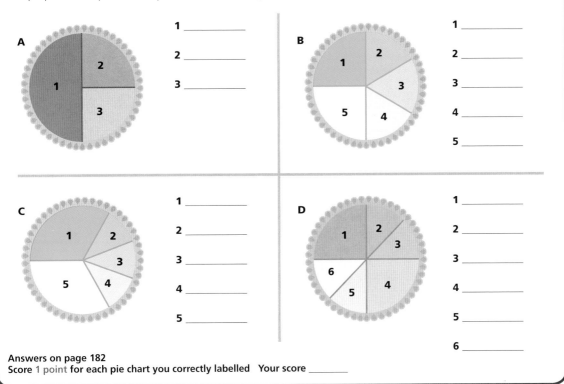

A

1 _____

2 _____

3 _____

B

1 _____

2 _____

3 _____

4 _____

5 _____

C

1 _____

2 _____

3 _____

4 _____

5 _____

D

1 _____

2 _____

3 _____

4 _____

5 _____

6 _____

Answers on page 182
Score 1 point for each pie chart you correctly labelled   Your score _____

13 STAR-STRUCK

Gazing out from the stage, you wonder what proportion of your audience are students on complimentary tickets. The theater holds 160 people, but it is only three-quarters full, and 90 of the audience members are students. What percentage of the audience is students?

Answer _____

Answer on page 182
Score 1 point for a correct answer   Your score _____

14 LITTLE BROTHER

A woman tells you that the average age of her three sons is eight, but they are all under 10. What is the youngest any of them can be?

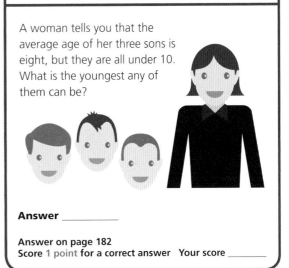

Answer _____

Answer on page 182
Score 1 point for a correct answer   Your score _____

15 CHEESE PLEASE

In the cheese store the offerings are priced per pound.
Can you calculate how much the following orders will cost?

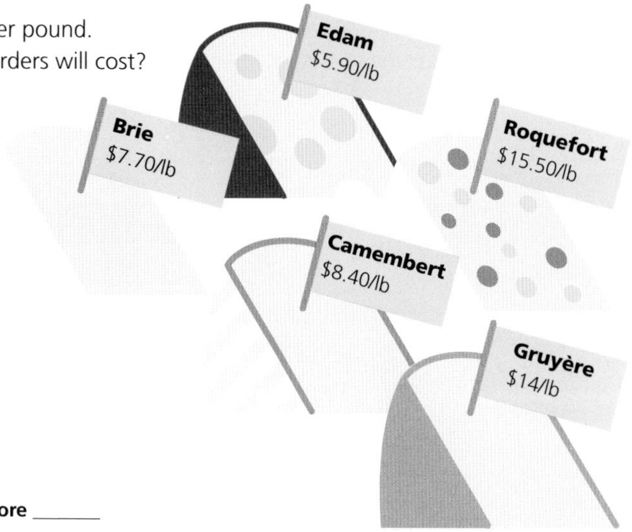

A 3oz Roquefort
12oz Gruyère _____

B 12oz Edam
8oz Roquefort
4oz Brie _____

C 4oz Camembert
6oz Roquefort
12oz Gruyère
3oz Edam _____

Edam
$5.90/lb

Brie
$7.70/lb

Roquefort
$15.50/lb

Camembert
$8.40/lb

Gruyère
$14/lb

Answers on page 182
Score 1 point for each correct answer   Your score _____

16 HENRY'S CAT

Henry is four years older than his cat, but eight years ago Henry was twice as old as his cat. How old is Henry?

Answer _____

Answer on page 182
Score 1 point for the correct answer   Your score _____

17 BILL BRAINTEASER

Your currency has bank bills in the denominations 5, 10, and 20. Given the number of bills in your wallet and their total value, can you figure out the lowest value note you could have in each case?

	Number of notes	Total value	Lowest value note
A	3	40	_____
B	4	40	_____
C	4	50	_____
D	5	60	_____

Answers on page 182
Score 1 point for each correct answer   Your score _____

18 WHAT TIME IS IT? I

A series of sequential numbers are grouped together by a base. For example, our normal counting system is base 10; we count from 0 to 9 as single digits, and 10, which means "one ten" and "zero single units." (So the number 210 means "two 100s," "one 10," and "no single units"). In everyday life we use bases when talking about the time. Hours, for instance, are in base 12, and minutes and seconds are in base 60. Practice using base 12 here:

A In 17 hours it will be 2am, what time is it now?

Answer _____

B In 16 hours you will be eight hours late for your 9am appointment. What time is it now?

Answer _____

C Stockholm is seven hours behind Singapore. If it is 11am in Singapore, what time will it be in Stockholm 16 hours from now?

Answer _____

D Melbourne is 16 hours ahead of New York, which is five hours behind London. Eric leaves Melbourne at 4pm local time and flies to London. According to his watch, which is on New York time, he touches down at 1pm. How long was his flight and what is the local time?

Answer _____

Answers on page 182
Score 1 point for each correct answer   Your score _____

19 WHAT TIME IS IT? II

Minutes are counted in base 60. Try using base 60 with the following:

A You finished a 10-mile run in 1 hour 12 minutes. Your running partner finished 24 minutes ahead of you. You both started at 10:11am. What time did your partner cross the finishing line?

Answer _____

B You are late for an appointment. The bus you are traveling on is 6 minutes delayed. You were already running 17 minutes late. It will take another 18 minutes to arrive at your destination. It is now 9:36am. What time is your appointment?

Answer _____

C The time is 4:48pm. You put the dinner in the oven to cook for 90 minutes, but have to check it at two equal intervals. At what times should you check?

Answer _____

D The film Hours and Minutes starts at 7:13pm in the Village Cinema. The same film is showing at 7:37pm at the City Cinema. Not including the 7-minute walk to the train station, it takes 12 minutes to get to the City and 21 minutes to get to the Village. The time is now 6:41pm. Which cinema can you arrive at first?

Answer _____

Answers on page 182
Score 1 point for each correct answer   Your score _____

20 MISSING NUMBER

Can you figure out the missing number?

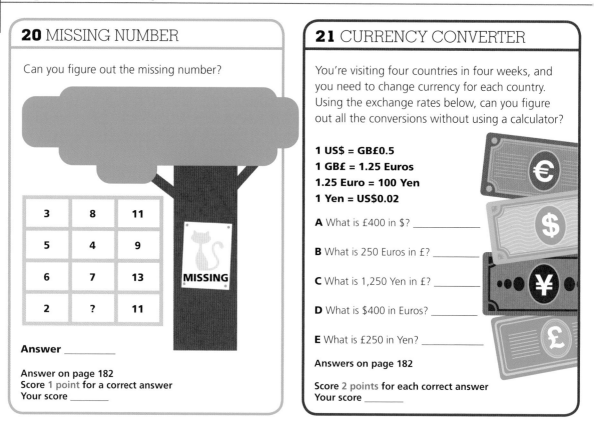

3	8	11
5	4	9
6	7	13
2	?	11

MISSING

Answer _____

Answer on page 182
Score **1 point** for a correct answer
Your score _____

21 CURRENCY CONVERTER

You're visiting four countries in four weeks, and you need to change currency for each country. Using the exchange rates below, can you figure out all the conversions without using a calculator?

1 US$ = GB£0.5
1 GB£ = 1.25 Euros
1.25 Euro = 100 Yen
1 Yen = US$0.02

A What is £400 in $? _____

B What is 250 Euros in £? _____

C What is 1,250 Yen in £? _____

D What is $400 in Euros? _____

E What is £250 in Yen? _____

Answers on page 182

Score **2 points** for each correct answer
Your score _____

22 WEIGHTS AND MEASURES

The metric system is quite easy to use when it comes to mental arithmetic, but the imperial system can be tougher. Using a calculator, can you convert from one to the other?

Remember:
1 kilogram = 2.2 pounds   **1 inch = 2.54 centimeters**
1 meter = 1.0936 yards   **1 ounce = 28.35 grams**
1 foot = 30.5 centimeters   **1 stone = 14 pounds**

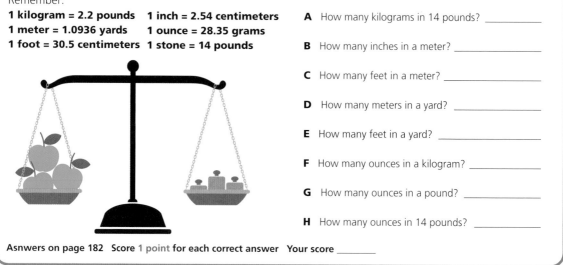

A   How many kilograms in 14 pounds? _____

B   How many inches in a meter? _____

C   How many feet in a meter? _____

D   How many meters in a yard? _____

E   How many feet in a yard? _____

F   How many ounces in a kilogram? _____

G   How many ounces in a pound? _____

H   How many ounces in 14 pounds? _____

Asnwers on page 182   Score 1 point for each correct answer   Your score _____

TIP

One way to improve at mental arithmetic is to keep practicing. This means working things out in your head every opportunity you get, rather than using a calculator. Set yourself mini-challenges by thinking up tough calculations (for example, 756 divided by 42) and working them out without writing anything down.

23 BARGAIN BIKE HUNTER

You are looking for a new bike, and you find the same model for sale at two stores, but at a different price in each one. You offer each store $200 for the bike. The first store says they'll split the difference and let you have the bike for halfway between your offer and the original price. The second store says they'll take off 20% from the original price and deduct another $10 on top. If the total of the two original asking prices was $750 and the total of the two final offers is $570, which store is offering the best price?

Answer _____

Answer on page 182
Score 1 point for the correct answer   Your score _____

24 DJ BATTLE

You asked Wilfred and Miles to DJ at your party, but you have only one album with 15 tracks on it. Wilfred wants to run a playlist that starts at track 4 and skips two tracks at a time. Miles wants to start his playlist near the end of the album and then work backward playing every fourth track, also resulting in a playlist four tracks long. If the total of the track numbers in Miles' playlist is six less than Wilfred's total, which track do they both like?

Answer _____

Answer on page 182
Score 1 point for the correct answer   Your score _____

Your score   **/70**    **60–70 GOLD**

You are skilled at mental arithmetic. Move on to the next chapter to see if you can meet the challenge of more advanced numerical reasoning puzzles.

30–59 SILVER

You are fairly numerate, but perhaps you struggled with some of the tougher questions. Try them again, using a paper and pen and a calculator if necessary. Learning how to calculate the correct answer is often most of the challenge with such problems— once you've cracked that, finding the answer is just a matter of mental arithmetic.

0–29 BRONZE

Numerical reasoning can be challenging, but don't let the mere sight of numbers send you into a tizzy. Try out the Challenge and practice mental arithmetic, then come back and try these exercises again.

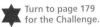

Turn to page 179 for the Challenge.

CHAPTER 9
THE FEAR OF
ALL CALCULATIONS
ADVANCED NUMERACY

The fear of all calculations

Although mathematics anxiety is a common problem, the puzzles in this chapter can be solved with the same reasoning and reflection as those in other chapters. Build up your confidence as you tackle them and you can overcome math anxiety.

QUESTIONNAIRE
Take this quick quiz to test your mathematical morale.

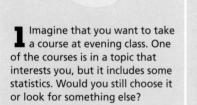

1 Imagine that you want to take a course at evening class. One of the courses is in a topic that interests you, but it includes some statistics. Would you still choose it or look for something else?

Choose it/No thanks
[score **1 point** for "Choose it"]

2 A friend is struggling to balance her bank statement and asks you to take a look at her checkbook. Would you be likely to agree or demur?

Agree/Demur
[score **1 point** for "Agree"]

3 On a team-building exercise you are assigned to work out the height of a tree using a long piece of string and a calculator. Would you try or rely on another team member rising to the challenge?

Have a go/Ask someone else
[score **1 point** for "Have a go"]

4 Your 12-year-old nephew asks for help with his math homework. Would you be willing to have a look or throw up your hands in horror?

Look/Horror
[score **1 point** for "Look"]

5 A society of which you are a member asks you to consider filling the post of treasurer. Would you be likely to give it a try or run a mile?

Try/Run
[score **1 point** for "Try"]

6 A real estate agent comes to value your house. She asks you to work out the area of the property in square feet. Would you be likely to succeed or fail?

Succeed/Fail
[score **1 point** for "Succeed"]

How did you score?
0–2: It seems you have a bad case of math anxiety. Try this chapter—the first few exercises at least. The more you exercise your numerical reasoning, the more confidence you will have to tackle tougher questions.

3–4: You are frightened of math. Put your faculties to the test with the exercises in this chapter.

5–6: Math holds no terrors for you. Test your mettle with the exercises in this chapter and see if you can do the toughest ones.

1 CALCULATOR CRISIS

The operators (+, −, x, and ÷) on your calculator are missing but you don't have time to buy a new one, so you decide to figure out which of the missing keys corresponds to which operation. You label the gaps A, B, C, and D and try out some calculations, with the following results:

4 **(A)** 3 gives the same as 6 **(B)** 6
2 **(C)** 2 is 4
2 **(D)** 2 is also 4
5 **(C)** 7 is less than 8 **(D)** 2
Which button is which?

A _____
B _____
C _____
D _____

Answers on page 182
Score 1 point if you got all the buttons correct.
Your score _____

2 PRIME TIME

Prime numbers are numbers that cannot be divided by any other number except 1 and themselves: 1, 2, 3, 5, 7, 11, and so on. Can you work out the next 10 prime numbers after 11?

Prime numbers _____

Answer on page 182
Score 3 points if you got them all correct.
Your score _____

3 SHARED SECRET

With your prime numbers at hand, what do the following numbers have in common?

25
35
51
77
119
143

Answer_____

Answer on page 182

Score 1 point for a correct answer
Your score _____

TIP

Try your hand at number-based puzzles in newspapers and magazines. Strictly speaking, puzzles such as Sudoku and Kakuro involve logical rather than numerical reasoning (although they feature numbers, they could equally feature any form of symbols), but there are other puzzle types you can find that exercise your numeracy, such as KenKen, number puzzles, "side-by-side," and "secret number."

4 AVERAGE APPLES

You are working at a fruit store and you take delivery of a crate of apples. You want to work out the average weight of an apple in the crate, but you only have the information shown on the label opposite. Can you work out the average weight of an apple in the crate?

Answer _____

Answer on page 182
Score 1 point for a correct answer
Your score _____

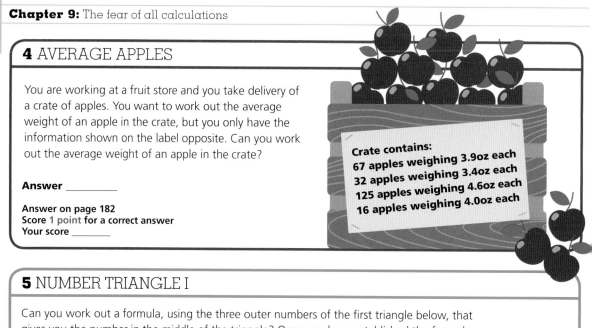

Crate contains:
67 apples weighing 3.9oz each
32 apples weighing 3.4oz each
125 apples weighing 4.6oz each
16 apples weighing 4.0oz each

5 NUMBER TRIANGLE I

Can you work out a formula, using the three outer numbers of the first triangle below, that gives you the number in the middle of the triangle? Once you have established the formula, use it to work out the missing number in the third triangle.

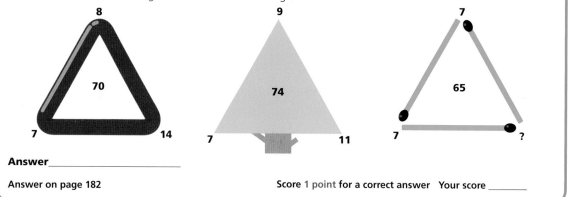

Answer_____

Answer on page 182

Score 1 point for a correct answer   Your score _____

6 NUMBER TRIANGLE II

What is the missing number?   **Answer on page 182**

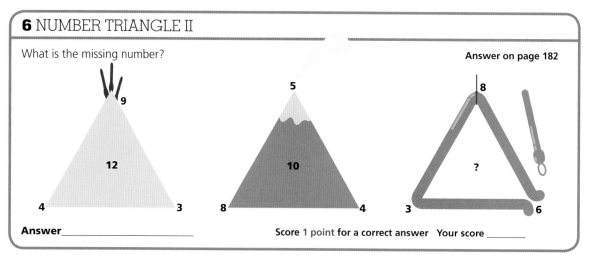

Answer_____   **Score 1 point** for a correct answer   Your score _____

7 NUMBER CROSS I

What is the missing number?

Answer on page 183

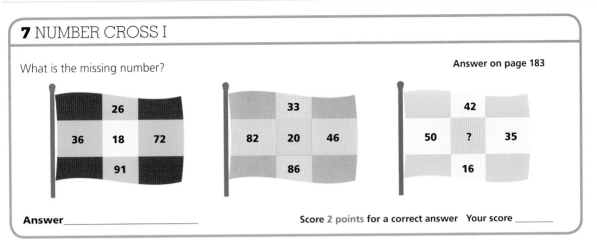

Answer_____

Score **2 points** for a correct answer   Your score _____

8 NUMBER CROSS II

What is the missing number?

Answer on page 183

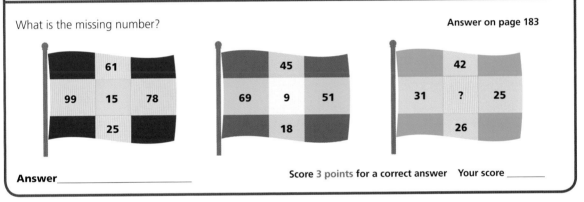

Answer_____

Score **3 points** for a correct answer   Your score _____

9 NUMBER PENTAGON

What are the missing numbers?

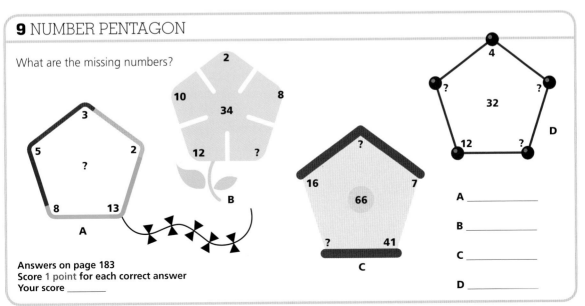

Answers on page 183
Score **1 point** for each correct answer
Your score _____

A _____

B _____

C _____

D _____

10 NUMBER SQUARE

What is the missing number?

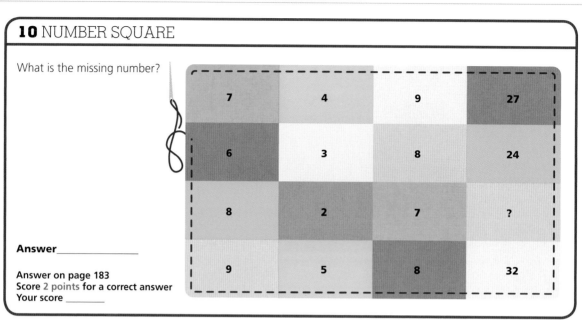

7	4	9	27
6	3	8	24
8	2	7	?
9	5	8	32

Answer_____

Answer on page 183
Score **2 points** for a correct answer
Your score _____

11 WHERE ANGLES FEAR TO TREAD

One of the basic principles of geometry is that the angles of a triangle add up to 180°. You may also recognize right-angle triangles—triangles in which one angle is 90°. Armed with this information, can you work out the missing angles in these triangles? Note these angles are not drawn to scale.

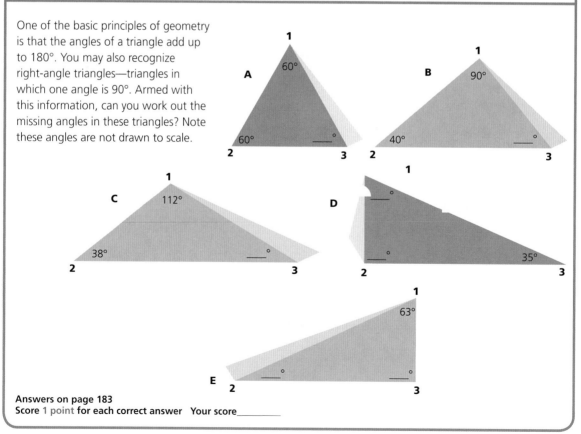

Answers on page 183
Score **1 point** for each correct answer   Your score_____

12 IN THE AREA

Here are some formulas for areas of two-dimensional shapes. Can you use them to work out the areas and volumes of the shapes given? For the purposes of this exercise, pi has a value of 3.14.

Area of a rectangle
= width x height

Area of a triangle
= ½ x base x height

Area of a circle
= pi x radius²
Circumference of a circle
= 2 x pi x radius

A

6
4

What is the area of this rectangle? _____

B

6
3

What is the area of this triangle? _____

C

5

This rectangle has an area of 20. What is its height?

_____

D

4

This triangle has an area of 8. What is its height?

_____

E

3

What are the area and circumference of this circle?

_____

F

8

What are the area and circumference of this circle?

_____

13 FLOOR SPACE

It's your first day on the job as a real estate agent and you are sent to measure a cottage. Can you use the floorplan below to figure out the total floor area of the house? Each square is 5 sq ft.

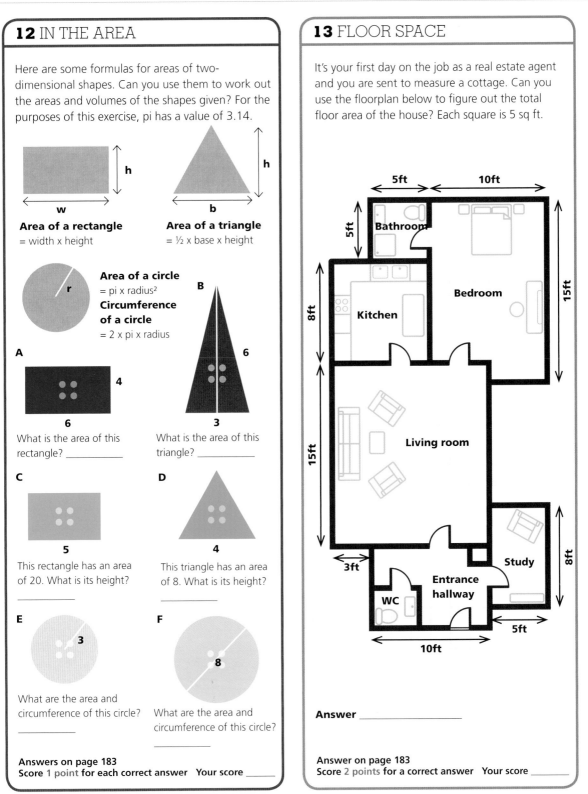

5ft   10ft

5ft Bathroom

8ft Kitchen   Bedroom   15ft

15ft Living room

3ft   Study   8ft

Entrance hallway

WC

5ft

10ft

Answer _____

14 ALGEBRA ALERT

Algebra is simpler than it looks and, without realizing, you are probably using it on a daily basis. Can you work out what the letter "a" equals in these simple equations?

A You've bought 7 apples for a total cost of $4.20. How much does each apple cost? **a x 7 = 420** _____

B Your designer tells you that three rolls of fabric will be enough to cover nine armchairs with 2 square yards of fabric each. How many square yards is each roll?
3a ÷ 9 = 2 _____

C Mrs. Thruppet donates four boxes of cat food to the pet rescue drive, and Mrs Roundel donates three boxes of cat food. The pet rescue ends up with 21 cans of cat food. How many cans were in each box? **4a + 3a = 21** _____

D Five equally crewed fishing boats left harbor last night, and although all the fishermen make it back alive, only three boats limped back into port the next morning, along with 10 bedraggled fishermen swimming behind them. How many fishermen crew each boat? **5a = 10 + 3a** _____

E Three packets of gum contain as many sticks of gum as 48 divided by the number of sticks of gum in a packet. How many sticks of gum are in a packet? **3a = 48 ÷ a** _____

Answers on page 183
Score 1 point for each correct answer
Your score _____

15 PLOT IT

Algebra comes in handy for describing lines on graphs. You can also turn real-life scenarios into graphs: any situation in which one variable changes according to another one, and numbers are involved, can be plotted. For instance, the algebraic equation x = y shows that every time one unit is added along the x axis, one unit is also added along the y axis (see graph below). Using a separate piece of graph paper, can you plot the lines that correspond to the simple equations that arise from these scenarios.

Line 1: You are bicycling up a steep hill, gaining 3 feet of altitude for every 6 feet you travel. Draw a graph representing the slope of the hill. **x = 2y**

Line 2: Your uneconomical car does 2 miles to the gallon. Plotting the distance (in miles) on the y axis and gallons of fuel on the x axis, graph out your cumulative fuel consumption with the distance as **2x = y**

Line 3: Your brother is two years older than you. Draw a graph of his age on the y axis against yours on the x axis. **y = x + 2**

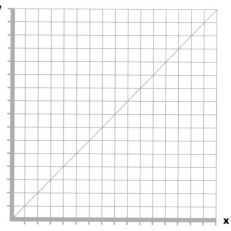

Answers on page 183
Score 1 point for each correct graph.
Your score _____

16 LEARNING CURVE

Simple algebraic equations can also be used to represent curved lines on graphs. For example, you could plot a graph of the width of a square carpet on the x axis against its area on the y axis: $y = x^2$. Every time the width, which is the x coordinate, increases by a unit, the area will increase by that unit squared and this will be the y coordinate. The graph below shows the curved line representing the equation $y = x^2$.

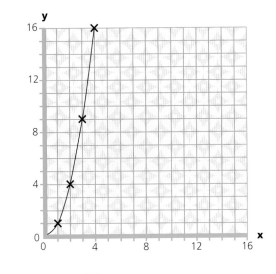

On a separate piece of graph paper, can you now draw a graph with the area of a square room plotted on the x axis and the width of the room on the y axis $y = x^2 - 2$.

Answer on page 183
Score 2 points for drawing the curve correctly

Your score _____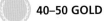

TIP

If you feel that topics such as algebra and geometry are alien, you might want to consider revisiting some basics. There are many websites you can visit that offer easy and engaging ways to reacquaint yourself with math, from the basics through more advanced mathematics, helping you build your confidence so you can tackle serious calculations without fear.

Your score   /50   **40–50 GOLD**   **20–39 SILVER**   **0–19 BRONZE**

Your mathematical skills are good but did you get 50 out of 50? If you didn't get some of the answers, can you work out where you went wrong?

You had a good crack at the questions but perhaps your math skills could do with a brush-up. Revisit the questions you got wrong.

Possibly your confidence is low, and perhaps you didn't try some of the exercises, or maybe you gave up on them too easily? Keep trying these puzzles until you can answer all of them.

Turn to page 179 for the Challenge.

CHAPTER 10
TIP OF THE TONGUE
VERBAL INTELLIGENCE

Tip of the tongue

Verbal acuity, or verbal intelligence, is the ability to use and understand words and language. Your ability results from a combination of your knowledge of language, such as your breadth of vocabulary, and your capability in applying it.

QUESTIONNAIRE
Use this quick quiz to get an overview of your verbal abilities.

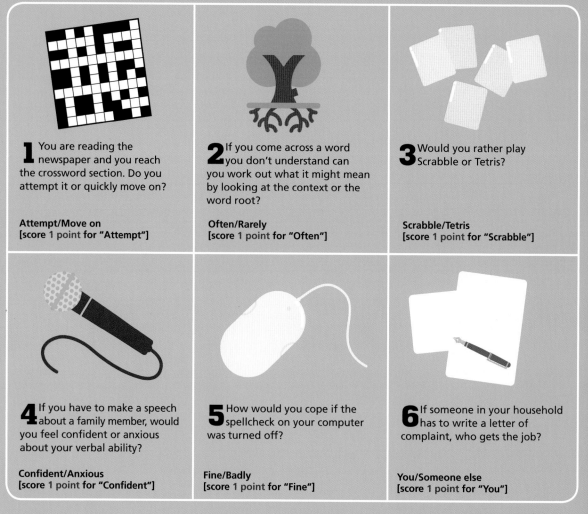

1 You are reading the newspaper and you reach the crossword section. Do you attempt it or quickly move on?

Attempt/Move on
[score 1 point for "Attempt"]

2 If you come across a word you don't understand can you work out what it might mean by looking at the context or the word root?

Often/Rarely
[score 1 point for "Often"]

3 Would you rather play Scrabble or Tetris?

Scrabble/Tetris
[score 1 point for "Scrabble"]

4 If you have to make a speech about a family member, would you feel confident or anxious about your verbal ability?

Confident/Anxious
[score 1 point for "Confident"]

5 How would you cope if the spellcheck on your computer was turned off?

Fine/Badly
[score 1 point for "Fine"]

6 If someone in your household has to write a letter of complaint, who gets the job?

You/Someone else
[score 1 point for "You"]

How did you score?
0–2: You have little or no confidence in your verbal acuity. Work through the exercises in this chapter to examine your verbal intelligence and give your verbal skills a thorough workout.
3–4: Your verbal intelligence is not bad, but there are areas you need to work on. Go through the exercises to find the areas you need to strengthen.
5–6: You are articulate and literate, but verbal intelligence and knowledge can always be improved—use the exercises in this chapter to test yourself and hone your abilities.

1 FROM A TO Z ⏱

Allow yourself 30 seconds to arrange these 10 words in alphabetical order. Write the appropriate number, from 1 to 10, next to each word.

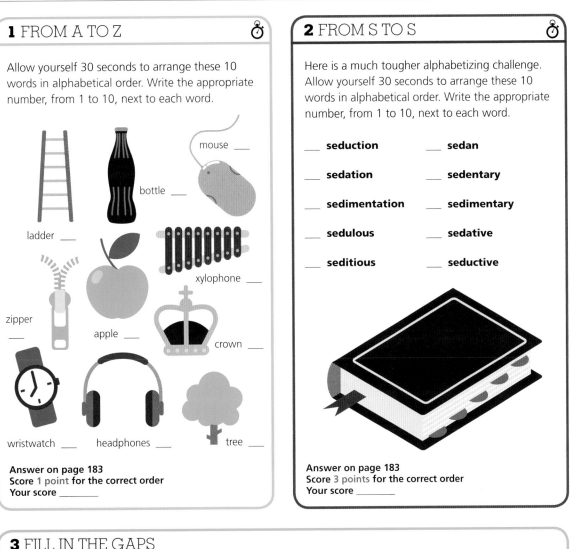

mouse ___

bottle ___

ladder ___

xylophone ___

zipper ___

apple ___

crown ___

wristwatch ___   headphones ___   tree ___

Answer on page 183
Score 1 point for the correct order
Your score _____

2 FROM S TO S ⏱

Here is a much tougher alphabetizing challenge. Allow yourself 30 seconds to arrange these 10 words in alphabetical order. Write the appropriate number, from 1 to 10, next to each word.

___ **seduction**   ___ **sedan**

___ **sedation**   ___ **sedentary**

___ **sedimentation**   ___ **sedimentary**

___ **sedulous**   ___ **sedative**

___ **seditious**   ___ **seductive**

Answer on page 183
Score 3 points for the correct order
Your score _____

3 FILL IN THE GAPS

Below is a story told in pictures. Can you place the words supplied on the right into the blank spaces so that they make sense and tell a story?

ignored; until; guarded; shook; squawking; but; arrived

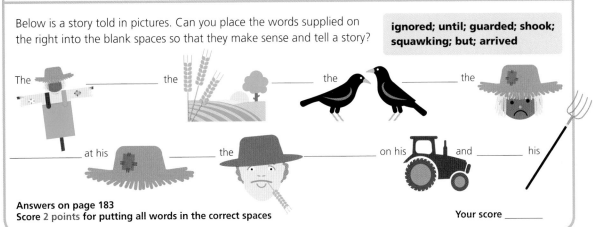

The _____ _____ the _____ _____ the _____ _____ the

_____ at his _____ the _____ on his _____ and _____ his

Answers on page 183
Score 2 points for putting all words in the correct spaces

Your score _____

4 SYNONYMS

Synonyms are words with the same or similar meaning. In the four lists of words below, circle the two that are the most similar in meaning.

A

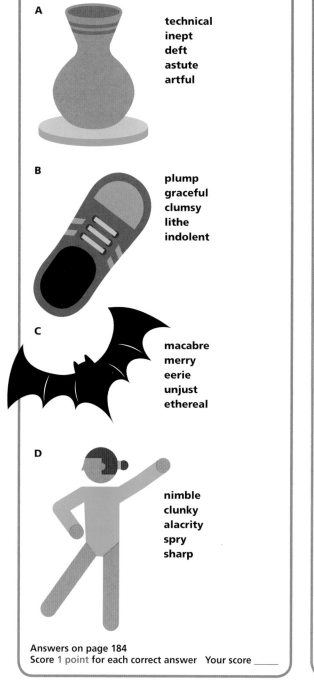

technical
inept
deft
astute
artful

B

plump
graceful
clumsy
lithe
indolent

C

macabre
merry
eerie
unjust
ethereal

D

nimble
clunky
alacrity
spry
sharp

Answers on page 184
Score **1 point** for each correct answer   Your score _____

5 SYNONYMS BY ANALOGY

In each of the following, circle the correct analogy that would make the statement true.

A

loneliness is
to **isolation** as
deception is to:
malice
mendacity
ingeniousness
errancy

B

robust is to **sturdy**
as **flimsy** is to:
heavy
feckless
fanciful
fragile

C

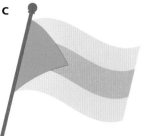

flag is to **pennant**
as **signal** is to:
waving
semaphore
alarmed
ignore

D

alert is to **ready**
as **honest** is to:
exhibition
pleasing
virtuous
circus

Answers on page 184
Score **1 point** for each correct answer   Your score _____

6 ANTONYMS

An antonym is a word that is opposite in meaning to another. In each of the lists below, circle the two words that are the most opposite in meaning.

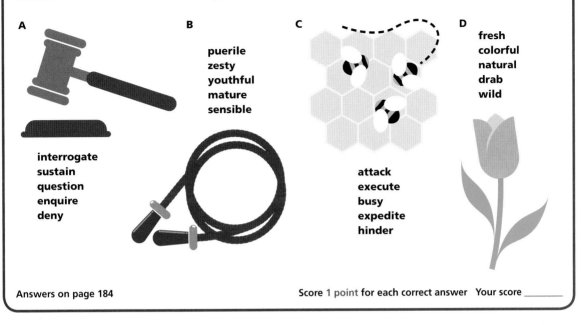

A

interrogate
sustain
question
enquire
deny

B

puerile
zesty
youthful
mature
sensible

C

attack
execute
busy
expedite
hinder

D

fresh
colorful
natural
drab
wild

Answers on page 184

Score **1 point** for each correct answer   Your score _____

7 ANTONYMS BY ANALOGY

In each of the following, circle the correct antonym that would make the statement true.

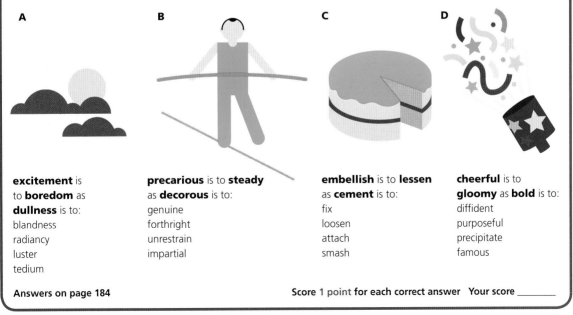

A

excitement is
to **boredom** as
dullness is to:
blandness
radiancy
luster
tedium

B

precarious is to **steady**
as **decorous** is to:
genuine
forthright
unrestrain
impartial

C

embellish is to **lessen**
as **cement** is to:
fix
loosen
attach
smash

D

cheerful is to
gloomy as **bold** is to:
diffident
purposeful
precipitate
famous

Answers on page 184

Score **1 point** for each correct answer   Your score _____

8 LETTER COUNTING

Here are 20 letters with their values. Using any number/combination of these letters, can you make words with these exact scores?

A 18 _____

B 23 _____

C 17 _____

D 8 _____

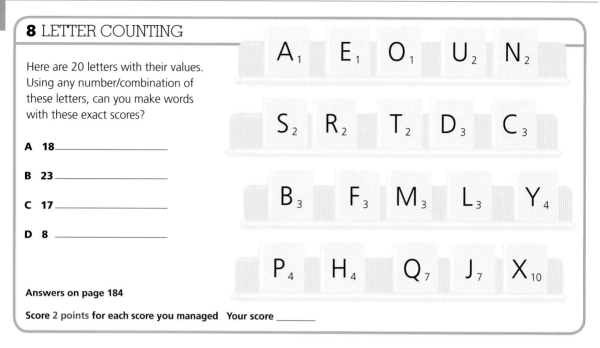

A_1 E_1 O_1 U_2 N_2

S_2 R_2 T_2 D_3 C_3

B_3 F_3 M_3 L_3 Y_4

P_4 H_4 Q_7 J_7 X_{10}

Answers on page 184

Score **2 points** for each score you managed   Your score _____

9 WORD GRID

Find the hidden 12-letter word by finding the starting letter and moving between adjacent letters in a horizontal or vertical direction only—no diagonal moves allowed. Use each letter only once. You need to guess any missing letters.

E	R	T	
V	P		V
E		T	E

Answer _____

Answer on page 184
Score **1 point** for a correct answer   Your score _____

10 ODD ONE OUT

A Which group of letters is the odd one out?

INGTRAIN
ILEMOB
FULSIN
PLAINFAST
GRAINWHOLE

Answer _____

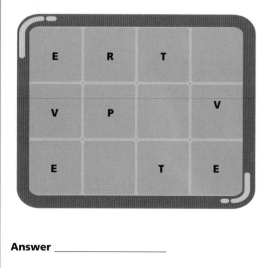

B Which group of letters here is the odd one out?

DHIP
DTAIR
OTAMINA
LMUDGE
YRINGE

Answer _____

Answers on page 184
Score **1 point** for each correct answer   Your score _____

11 STROOP TEST

The Stroop Test is a fun verbal assessment of how your perception and verbal intelligence work together, showing how unconscious processing can interfere with and even override your conscious intentions. On the right is a box of paint colors, but the words themselves are in a different color. Try saying aloud, as fast as you can, the color of each word, not what the word actually says. The part of your brain that processes the meaning of a word still works without your conscious intention, even when you are trying to think and say something else—in this case, what color the word is written in.

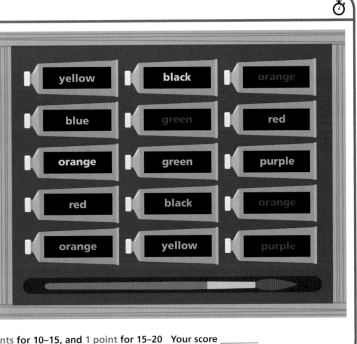

Score 3 points for less than 10 seconds, **2 points** for 10–15, and **1 point** for 15–20   Your score _____

12 UPSIDE-DOWN READING

Reading upside down text is a good way to stretch your ability to recognize letters and words, and makes a useful exercise for sharpening your verbal acuity. Without turning it round, quickly scan the passage on the right once and then cover it and answer the questions below.

The Musée du Louvre has a history extending back to medieval times. First constructed as a fortress in 1190 by King Philippe-Auguste to protect Paris against Viking raids, it lost its imposing keep in the reign of François I, who replaced it with a Renaissance-style building. Thereafter, four centuries of kings and emperors improved and enlarged it. A glass pyramid designed by I. M. Pei was added in 1989.

A What was the Louvre's original purpose?   _____

B Which king changed the building to Renaissance-style?   _____

C Who designed the glass pyramid?   _____

Answers on page 184

Score **1 point** for each correct answer   Your score _____

13 WORD LADDERS

Get from the word on the bottom rung to the word on the top rung by changing one letter at a time to form a new (real) word for each rung of the ladder. For instance, you could get from GLUM to FREE by going GLUM > GLUE > FLUE> FLEE > FREE. Time yourself how long it takes to get from the bottom of the ladder to the top.

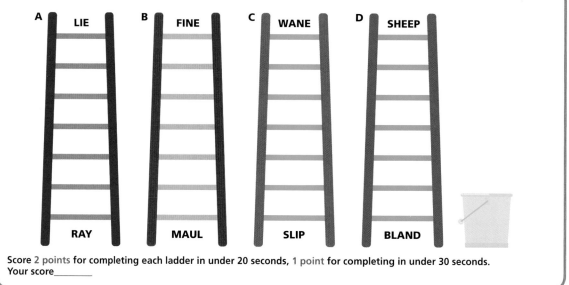

A LIE

B FINE

C WANE

D SHEEP

RAY

MAUL

SLIP

BLAND

Score **2 points** for completing each ladder in under 20 seconds, **1 point** for completing in under 30 seconds.
Your score_____

14 WORDS WITHIN WORDS

How many words of three or more letters can you make in 5 minutes by using letters from each of the the long words below?

professional

creationism

illustrated

admittance

peregrination

rhetorical

**Total number
of words** _____

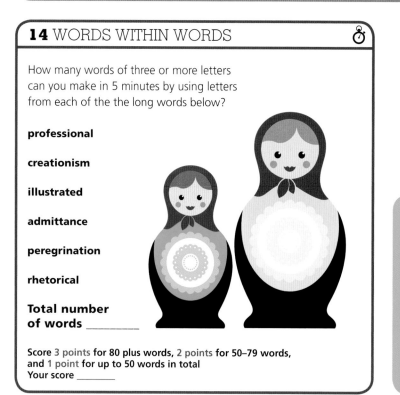

Score **3 points** for 80 plus words, **2 points** for 50–79 words, and **1 point** for up to 50 words in total
Your score _____

TIP

A good way to continually increase the breadth of your vocabulary is to make a point of learning at least one new word every day. Whenever you come across a new word, look it up and then make sure you use it in a sentence as often as you can to help fix it firmly in your memory.

15 FRUIT SALAD

Which one of these is not an anagram of a fruit? Unscramble all the anagrams to discover which is the odd one out.

A ANA BAN

B FARE PIG RUT

C A CRUEL WOLF I

D EARN MET OWL

E TRACK CAN BLUR

F PLAIN PEEP

G ELECT MEN IN

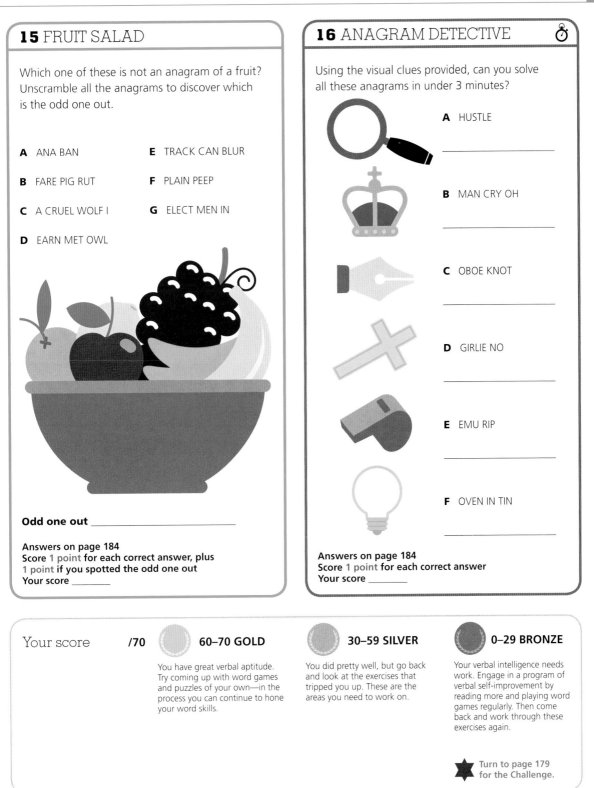

Odd one out _____

Answers on page 184
Score 1 point for each correct answer, plus
1 point if you spotted the odd one out
Your score _____

16 ANAGRAM DETECTIVE

Using the visual clues provided, can you solve all these anagrams in under 3 minutes?

A HUSTLE

_____

B MAN CRY OH

_____

C OBOE KNOT

_____

D GIRLIE NO

_____

E EMU RIP

_____

F OVEN IN TIN

_____

Answers on page 184
Score 1 point for each correct answer
Your score _____

Your score   /70

60–70 GOLD
You have great verbal aptitude. Try coming up with word games and puzzles of your own—in the process you can continue to hone your word skills.

30–59 SILVER
You did pretty well, but go back and look at the exercises that tripped you up. These are the areas you need to work on.

0–29 BRONZE
Your verbal intelligence needs work. Engage in a program of verbal self-improvement by reading more and playing word games regularly. Then come back and work through these exercises again.

Turn to page 179 for the Challenge.

CHAPTER 11
LOST IN SPACE
VISUO-SPATIAL INTELLIGENCE

Lost in space

Visuo-spatial intelligence or aptitude is the form of intelligence you use when thinking about physical shapes, distances, angles, and sizes in the real world. You use this for example when packing cans into a cabinet or when playing games such as Tetris.

QUESTIONNAIRE
Do this quick quiz to see how visuo-spatially aware you are.

1 Would you be able to fit differently shaped items into a small cabinet, or would you just hope they don't fall out when you next open the cabinet door?

Fit/Fall out
[score 1 point for "Fit"]

2 If you were driving your car and you came to a narrow passage not much wider than your vehicle, would you risk it or find a different route?

Risk/Avoid
[score 1 point for "Risk"]

3 When using a map to find your way, do you have to turn the map around to line up with the streets or can you do the rotation in your head?

Turn map round/Rotate in head
[score 1 point for "Rotate in head"]

4 You're ordering a new carpet, but the salesman needs to know the approximate floor area of your living room. Would you try to estimate it or would you need to get out the tape measure?

Estimate/Measure
[score 1 point for "Estimate"]

5 You're out hiking with a friend and he unfolds the map to check your location, then hands it back to you for folding. Will the map end up perfectly pressed or folded roughly?

Pressed/Roughly
[score 1 point for "Pressed"]

6 The sun is out and you set up the deckchair. Can you snap it into shape without difficulty, or will you have to wrestle with it like an angry anaconda?

Snap/Wrestle
[score 1 point for "Snap"]

How did you score?
0–2: Sounds as though you're struggling a little with your visuo-spatial intelligence. Work through all the exercises to help improve your ability.

3–4: Your visuo-spatial intelligence is average, but you sometimes lack confidence. Use the exercises in this chapter to put your visuo-spatial acuity through its paces and prove that you can do it.

5–6: You have an acute sense of visuo-spatial awareness. Put your capacity to the test and see if you can complete all the challenges in the chapter without too much pondering.

1 SPOT THE DIFFERENCE

Below are two apparently identical pictures. In fact, there are six differences between
the two—can you spot them all? Time how long it takes you.

Answer on page 184

Less than 1 minute: score **3 points**, less than 2 minutes: **2 points**, more than 2 minutes: **1 point**   **Your score** _____

2 FLOOR PLANNER

You have a new job as a carpet layer. If each square on the floorplan below is 5 sq ft, can you
work out how many square feet of carpet in total you will need for the rooms? The hall and
the stairs are to remain uncarpeted.

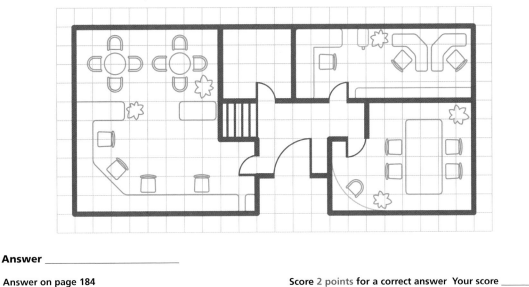

Answer _____

Answer on page 184   Score **2 points** for a correct answer **Your score** _____

3 GET YOUR HEAD AROUND THIS

Mental rotation (the ability to turn an image in your mind's eye accurately enough so that you can correctly perceive its elements relative to one another) is a key marker of visuo-spatial aptitude, and is a popular puzzle in IQ tests. Here is a relatively simple example to get you started. These squares are identical but rotated, with one exception. Which is the odd one out?

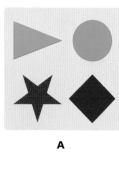
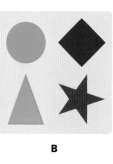

| A | B | C | D |

Answer _____ Answer on page 184 Score **1 point** for a correct answer Your score _____

4 AMBASSADORIAL AMBUSH

Now challenge your mental rotation ability further. As the new ambassador for Ruritania, you are hosting your first diplomatic function, but the etiquette department has placed the flags the wrong way around, and slipped in one from a different country for good measure. Below is what the Ruritanian flag looks like the right way around. Which of the flags on the right is the not the Ruritanian flag?

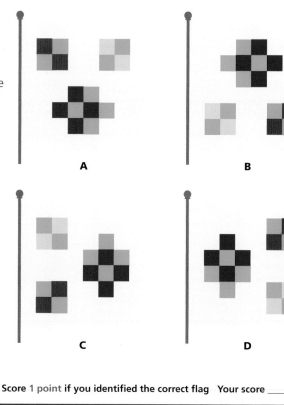

Answer _____ Answer on page 184 Score **1 point** if you identified the correct flag Your score _____

5 TOUGH ROTATION

Here is a more taxing mental rotation test. Which of the pentagons below is the odd one out?

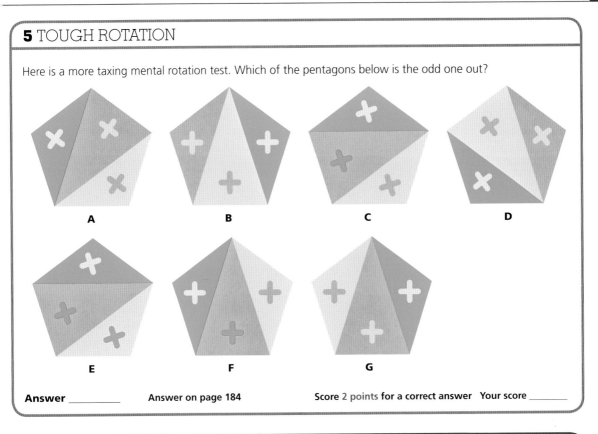

Answer _____   Answer on page 184   Score **2 points** for a correct answer   Your score _____

6 ABOUT FACE

Below are three views of the same cube. Use your mental rotation ability to work out which side is opposite pattern D?

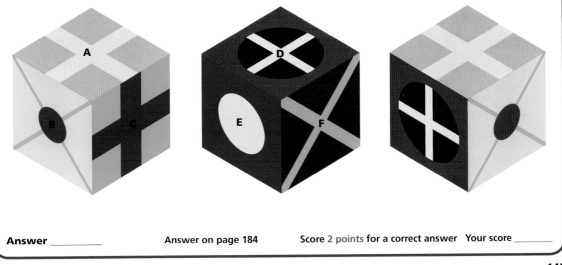

Answer _____   Answer on page 184   Score **2 points** for a correct answer   Your score _____

7 A CUBE WITH A VIEW

Which of the cubes below is not a view of the same cube?

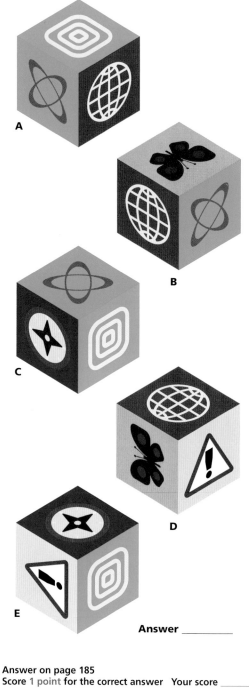

A

B

C

D

E

Answer _____

8 UNPACKING

If you "unfold" the sides of a cube, laying them flat to make a two-dimensional shape, you get a cross shape such as the one shown below.

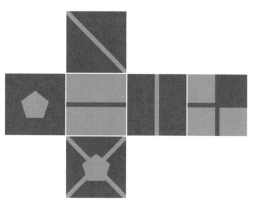

Which of the following is the cube that you can make by folding up this cross?

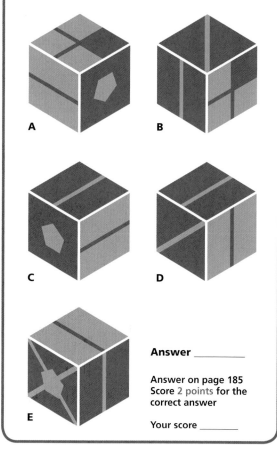

A

B

C

D

E

Answer _____

Answer on page 185
Score 2 points for the correct answer

Your score _____

TIP

Three-dimensional mental rotation can be quite a challenge. One way to cope is to break down the problem into more manageable aspects. For instance, when dealing with a cube, pick a face and label it in your mind as "top," then note the relationship between the top face and the ones on either side of it. Do the same with other views, so that all you are trying to visualize at any one time is the relationship between three elements.

9 WHERE IN THE WORLD?

You are hiking in the mountains. The picture below shows the view you can see. Based on the features and topography visible, can you locate yourself on the map beneath it?

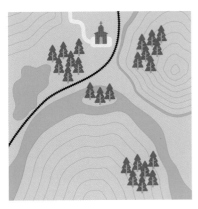

Answer on page 185
Score 2 points if you located yourself correctly
Your score _____

10 MAP MAKER

Using this list of landmarks and the links between them listed below, can you draw an accurate map?

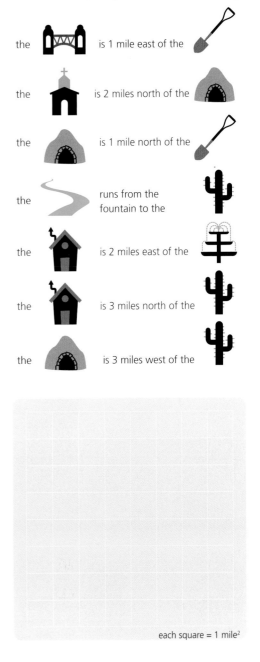

the ▦ is 1 mile east of the 🔨

the ⛪ is 2 miles north of the ⛰

the ⛰ is 1 mile north of the 🔨

the 〰 runs from the fountain to the

the 🏠 is 2 miles east of the ⛲

the 🏠 is 3 miles north of the 🌵

the ⛰ is 3 miles west of the 🌵

each square = 1 mile²

Answer on page 185
Score 2 points if your map is accurate   Your score _____

11 FREEZER PACKER

A load of shopping has just been delivered, and you have the unenviable task of cramming it into the freezer. Can you work out the best configuration and sketch the shapes of the packages below onto the diagram of the freezer?

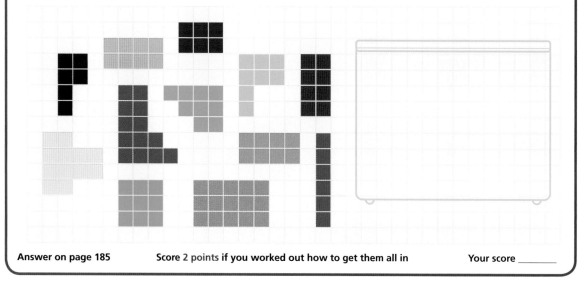

Answer on page 185   **Score 2 points if you worked out how to get them all in**   Your score _____

12 TILE GAME

You have a tile game where any adjacent tile can be moved up or down into the empty space. It currently looks like this:

Which of the following can't you make?

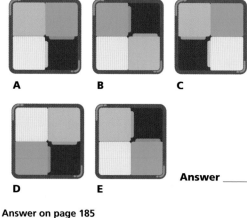

A   **B**   **C**

D   **E**

Answer _____

Answer on page 185
Score 1 point for a correct answer Your score _____

13 CHESS MOVES

The key on the left shows a knight chess piece can move to any of the squares indicated with a black dot. On the board below, what is the least number of moves needed for the knight to take the stationary rook?

8
7
6
5
4
3
2
1
  A B C D E F G H

Answer
_____

Answer on page 185
Score 1 point for a correct answer Your score _____

14 SHAPES SERIES I

Look at the following sequence of four and decide which of the three options below comes next in the series.

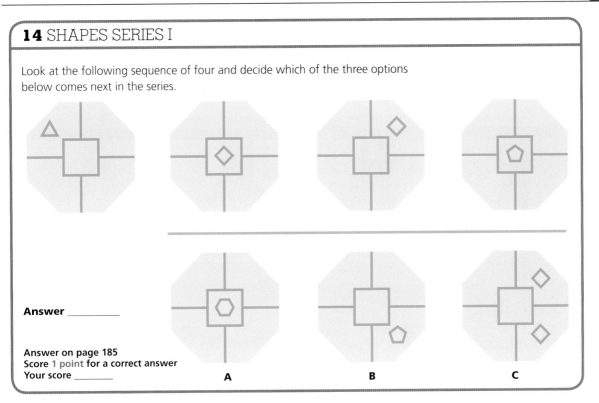

Answer _____

Answer on page 185
Score 1 point for a correct answer
Your score _____

A   B   C

15 SHAPES SERIES II

The four strips below on the left each show the same sequence. Which sequence on the right will continue the series?

Answer _____

Answer on page 185
Score 1 point for a correct answer   Your score _____

16 STRIKE A POSE

Look at the sequence of movements.

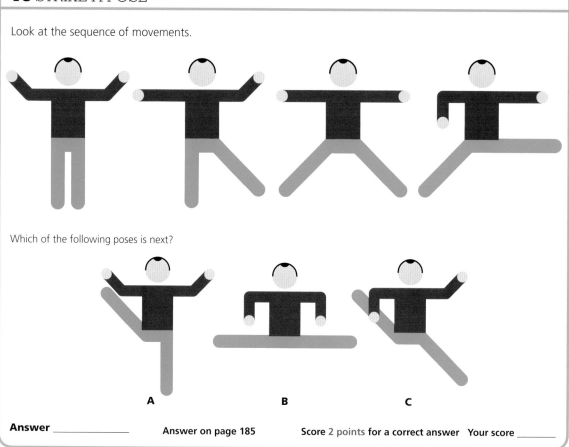

Which of the following poses is next?

A   B   C

Answer _____   Answer on page 185   Score 2 points **for a correct answer** Your score _____

17 TELLTALE SHAPES I

Look at the series of shapes below. The colors tell you something about the shapes.

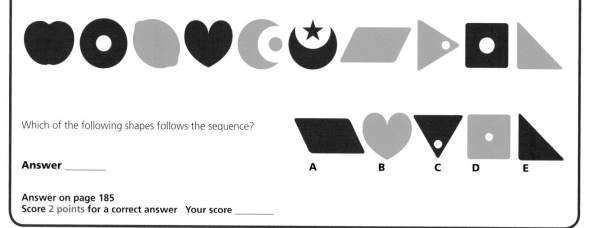

Which of the following shapes follows the sequence?

Answer _____

A   B   C   D   E

Answer on page 185
Score 2 points **for a correct answer** Your score _____

18 TELLTALE SHAPES II

Look at the sequence on the right.

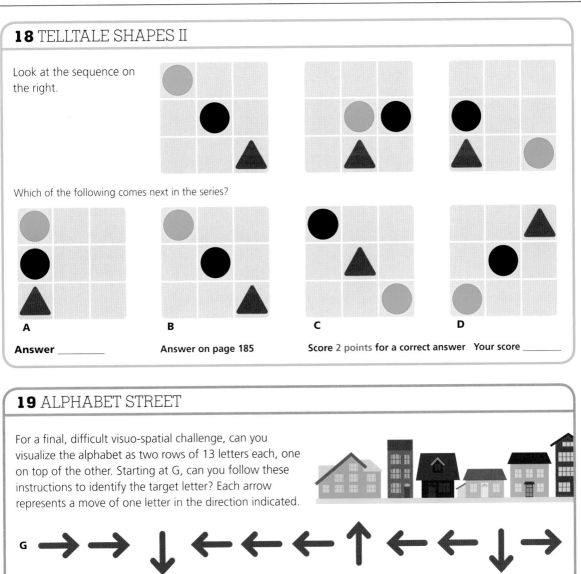

Which of the following comes next in the series?

A
B
C
D

Answer _____
Answer on page 185
Score 2 points for a correct answer **Your score** _____

19 ALPHABET STREET

For a final, difficult visuo-spatial challenge, can you visualize the alphabet as two rows of 13 letters each, one on top of the other. Starting at G, can you follow these instructions to identify the target letter? Each arrow represents a move of one letter in the direction indicated.

G → → ↓ ← ← ← ↑ ← ← ↓ →

Answer _____
Answer on page 186
Score 4 points for a correct answer **Your score** _____

Your score **/40**

30–40 GOLD

Your performance on these exercises is impressive. Take a look at the ones where you stumbled and work on those aspects of visuo-spatial intelligence.

20–29 SILVER

Some of the tougher exercises caused you problems. Go back and work through them again. Familiarize yourself with this sort of puzzle to try to improve your performance.

0–19 BRONZE

Mental rotation puts your head in a spin. Check out the Challenge to see how you can work on your visuo-spatial aptitude in everyday life.

Turn to page 179 for the Challenge

Logic jam

Logical intelligence involves your powers of reasoning—thinking through problems in a methodical, step-by-step way. However, the human brain is not wired for this kind of thinking, so most people use intuition and mental shortcuts in reasoning. A key to success in logic tests is to think about the exact wording of the question.

QUESTIONNAIRE
Can you avoid logical fallacies and see through codes and cyphers, or do you tend to stumble into logical pitfalls and struggle to break codes? Use this quick quiz to find out how logical your brain is.

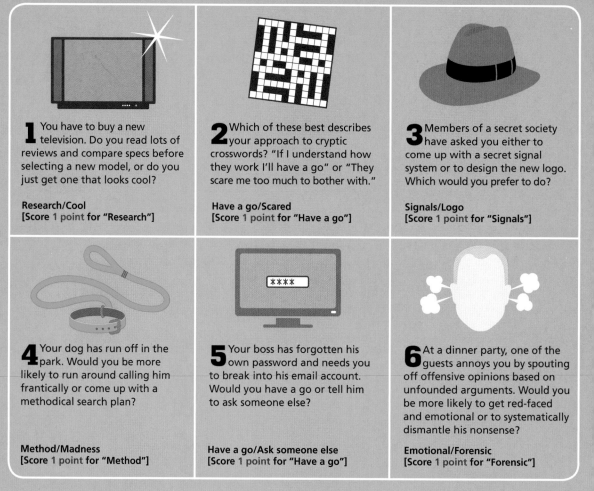

1 You have to buy a new television. Do you read lots of reviews and compare specs before selecting a new model, or do you just get one that looks cool?

Research/Cool
[Score 1 point for "Research"]

2 Which of these best describes your approach to cryptic crosswords? "If I understand how they work I'll have a go" or "They scare me too much to bother with."

Have a go/Scared
[Score 1 point for "Have a go"]

3 Members of a secret society have asked you either to come up with a secret signal system or to design the new logo. Which would you prefer to do?

Signals/Logo
[Score 1 point for "Signals"]

4 Your dog has run off in the park. Would you be more likely to run around calling him frantically or come up with a methodical search plan?

Method/Madness
[Score 1 point for "Method"]

5 Your boss has forgotten his own password and needs you to break into his email account. Would you have a go or tell him to ask someone else?

Have a go/Ask someone else
[Score 1 point for "Have a go"]

6 At a dinner party, one of the guests annoys you by spouting off offensive opinions based on unfounded arguments. Would you be more likely to get red-faced and emotional or to systematically dismantle his nonsense?

Emotional/Forensic
[Score 1 point for "Forensic"]

How did you score?
0–2: You tend to think with your heart not your head, but do not despair. Many logical-thinking techniques can be learned easily through practice. If you struggle, try to learn from your mistakes.

3–4: You try to approach problems logically, but sometimes you fall into the trap of irrational thinking. Try to bear in mind that gut instinct can lead you astray.
5–6: You are as logical as Spock, but can you master all the challenges in this chapter?

1 WHICH ANIMAL IS NEXT?

The four animals below follow a sequence.

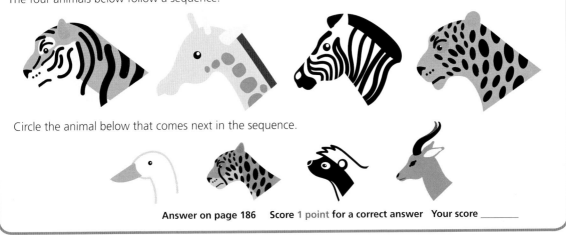

Circle the animal below that comes next in the sequence.

Answer on page 186   Score 1 point for a correct answer   Your score _____

2 MATERIAL WORLD

Which of the options listed on the right is the most logical one to continue this sequence?

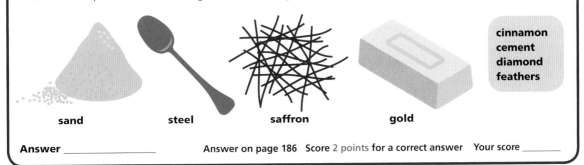

sand   steel   saffron   gold

cinnamon
cement
diamond
feathers

Answer _____   Answer on page 186   Score 2 points for a correct answer   Your score _____

3 THE DAY TODAY

The day before the day before yesterday is three days after Saturday. What day is it today?

Answer _____

Answer on page 186   Score 1 point for a correct answer   Your score _____

4 ALPHABET DIRECTIONS

Look at the letters below. Circle the letter that is to the right of the letter third to the left of the letter that (in the alphabet) comes after the letter that, below, is second to the left of T?

R   H   V   Y   S   A   I   T   B   N

Answer _____   Answer on page 186   Score **1 point** **for a correct answer**   **Your score** _____

5 REASONING BY ANALOGY

Select the number below that best completes the analogy **9** is to **6** as **12** is to…?

A 6

B 10

C -12

D 8

E 4

Answer _____   Answer on page 186   Score **1 point** **for a correct answer**   **Your score** _____

6 PEACE MAKER

165135 is to **peace** as **129225** is to:

A plenty

B love

C live

D abacus

Answer _____

Answer on page 186
Score **1 point** **for a correct answer**   **Your score** _____

7 COFFEE TIME

Coffee is to **5566153** as **apple** is to:

A 193572

B 51216161

C 216169

D 1937722

Answer _____

Answer on page 186
Score **1 point** **for a correct answer**   **Your score** _____

8 LAW AND ORDER

Arrange the words below in a logical sequence.

arrest

parole

prison

crime

court

thief

Answer _____

_____

Answer on page 186
Score 1 point for a correct answer   Your score _____

9 ANIMAL PLANET

Arrange the words below in a logical order.

mammal

beaver

herbivore

animal

vertebrate

rodent

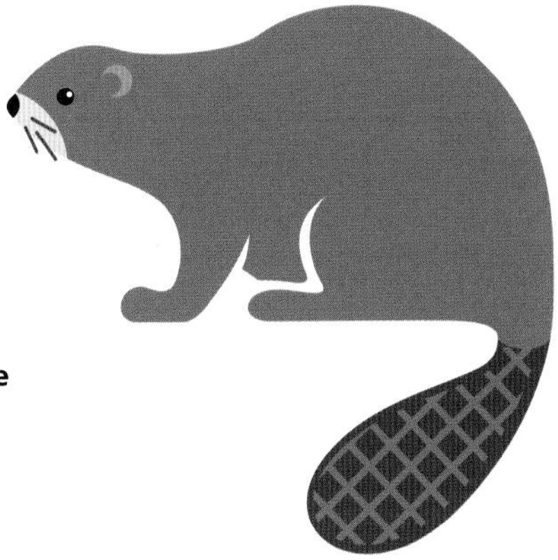

Answer _____

_____

Answer on page 186
Score 1 point for a correct answer   Your score _____

10 AIR AND SEA

Arrange the words below in a logical order.

dinghy

kite

submarine

jet

blimp

hydrofoil

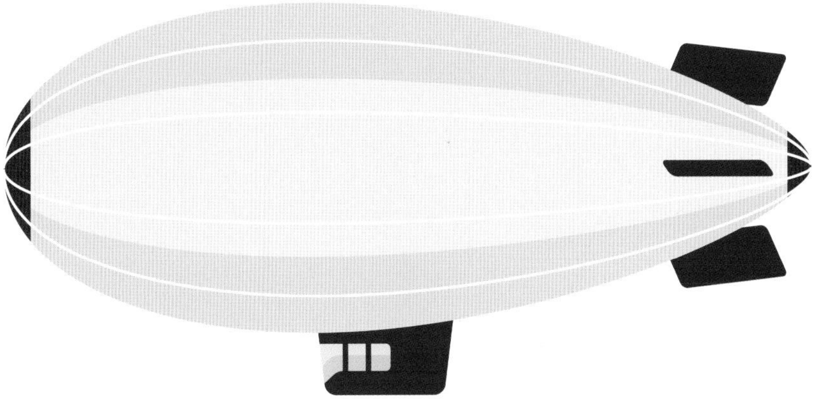

Answer _____

Answer on page 186   Score 1 point for a correct answer   Your score _____

11 MUSICIANS' UNION

These Venn diagrams represent an orchestra. The circle labeled C represents players of string instruments. The circle labeled U represents musicians who are members of a union. The head of the union plays a tuba. In which of the diagrams does the shaded area include him?

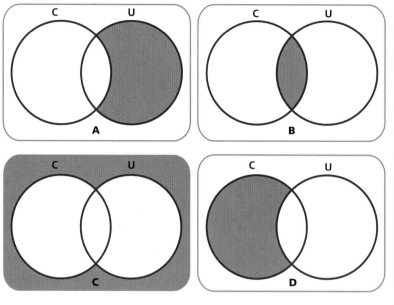

Answer _____ **Answer on page 186 Score 1 point for a correct answer Your score** _____

12 SPORTS CLUB

All the kids at sports club play at least one of the three sports offered: soccer, tennis, or volleyball. On the Venn diagram, shade in the areas that show children who either play one sport only, or those who play all three.

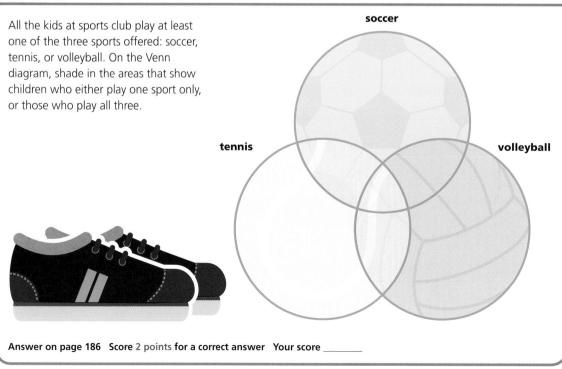

Answer on page 186 Score 2 points for a correct answer Your score _____

13 INTERVIEW CHOICE

There are 20 people who have applied for a job. Of these, 15 are women and 8 are shortlisted. Everyone who applied is either a woman or has been shortlisted. How many women were shortlisted? Drawing a Venn diagram on a separate piece of paper can help you work out the answer.

Answer _____

Answer on page 186
Score 2 points for a correct answer Your score _____

14 DAMAGED GOODS

At an auction you buy a job lot of 20 vinyl records, which are a mixture of albums and singles, but 6 of them are scratched. Of the records, 8 are albums. If there are 8 singles that are not scratched, how many of the albums are scratched? Drawing a Venn diagram on a separate piece of paper can help you work out the answer.

Answer _____

Answer on page 186
Score 2 points for a correct answer Your score _____

15 PIRATE SHIP

Out of 32 suspects captured from a pirate's ship:

5 pirates were arrested for wearing an eyepatch, having a wooden leg, and carrying a parrot on their shoulders.

3 pirates were arrested for wearing an eyepatch, having a wooden leg, but didn't carry a parrot on their shoulders.

9 pirates were not arrested for wearing an eyepatch, did not have a wooden leg, and didn't carry a parrot on their shoulders.

11 pirates were arrested for wearing an eyepatch and carried a parrot on their shoulders.

16 pirates were arrested for wearing an eyepatch.

9 pirates with wooden legs carried a parrot on their shoulders.

13 pirates had a wooden leg.

How many pirates carried a parrot on their shoulder?
Draw a Venn diagram on a separate piece of paper to work out the answer.

Answer _____   **Answer on page 186   Score 3 points for a correct answer Your score** _____

16 TRUE OR FALSE? I

Either Suzy has a driving license or Suzy isn't allowed to drive. Suzy doesn't have a license, so she isn't allowed to drive.

True or false?

Answer _____

Answer on page 186
Score 1 point for a correct answer   Your score _____

17 TRUE OR FALSE? II

If I am shorter than Bill, then Bill is tall. Bill is tall. Therefore I am shorter than Bill.

True or false?

Answer _____

Answer on page 186
Score 1 point for a correct answer   Your score _____

18 TRUE OR FALSE? III

At the school concert some of the students are playing in the orchestra. The students who are in the orchestra are musically gifted. Some of the students will go on to study at the Conservatory. Students who win a place at the Conservatory are musically gifted. Based solely on these statements, students who are playing in the orchestra will go on to study at the Conservatory.

True or false?

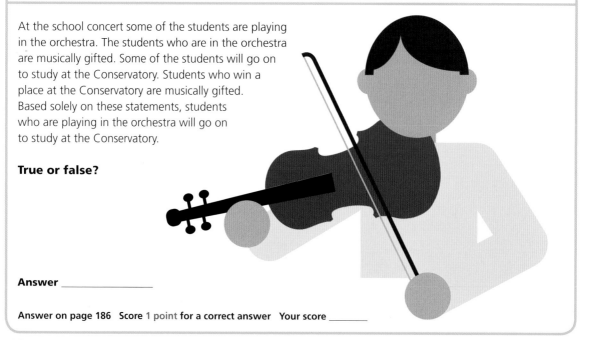

Answer _____

Answer on page 186   Score 1 point for a correct answer   Your score _____

19 WHICH IS NEXT?

SPARKLE   **LANGUISH**   **STUDENT**   **NEPOTISM**   **SECURE**

Which of the following words should come next?

IRRADIATE

REGULAR

MEDICAL

FINISHED

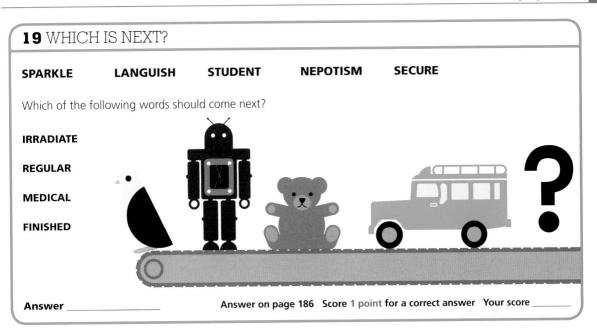

Answer _____

Answer on page 186   Score 1 point for a correct answer   Your score _____

20 LETTER LOGIC I

Circle the group of letters that is the odd one out.

BCDFGH

STUWXY

EFGIJK

DEFIJK

MNOQRS

Answer _____

Answer on page 186
Score 1 point for a correct answer   Your score _____

21 LETTER LOGIC II

Circle the group of letters that is the odd one out.

QRTYP

FGHKL

QDVHO

ZVBNM

ASDJL

Answer _____

Answer on page 186
Score 2 points for a correct answer   Your score _____

22 MEDAL CONFUSION

Your friends Tanya and Brendan have just come back from a sports event and are telling you about who won the medals in the 800m final, but they seem a little confused. Tanya says that Owembe got the gold and Beaker got the silver, but Brendan insists that Armitage won the gold and Owembe got the silver. It turns out that while Owembe, Beaker, and Armitage did indeed share the three medals, neither Tanya nor Brendan was completely accurate—each got one of the medals right and one wrong. Who actually won each of the medals?

Gold _____

Silver _____

Bronze _____

Answer on page 186   Score 2 points for a correct answer   Your score _____

23 WHICH CARD?

Look at the four cards below. You are not allowed to turn over more than two of them. Which should you turn over to find out whether the following hypothesis is true: "Of the cards shown, any card with a vowel on one side has an even number on the other side."

E

6

9

F

Answer _____

Answer on page 186   Score 2 points for a correct answer   Your score _____

24 SOCK SELECTOR

You have 20 pairs of socks: 10 pairs of purple socks and 10 pairs of red socks. However, they are not paired up, meaning that there are 40 loose socks in your sock drawer. With your eyes closed, how many socks do you need to pull out of the drawer to ensure that you end up with at least one matched pair?

Answer _____

Answer on page 186
Score 1 point for a correct answer   Your score _____

25 FESTIVE FOUL-UP

You've bought three boxes of chocolates as presents for your grandmother, uncle, and niece: a box of toffee centers for your niece, who is allergic to alcohol; a box of chocolate liqueurs for granny, who doesn't like toffee; and a mixed box for your uncle, who likes both. Disaster strikes, however, because the chocolate store has put the wrong labels on all three boxes. You don't want to ruin the packaging more than necessary, but neither do you want to give the wrong box to the wrong person. Which box or boxes should you open so that you can try a chocolate, in order to make sure everyone gets the right present?

Answer _____

Answer on page 187
Score 2 points for a correct answer   Your score _____

26 LETTER CHANGER

Letter substitution can be used when code writing (see Caesar Cipher, below), but can also be used for a simple word puzzle. In the example below, for the words on either side of the blank space the same letter can be used to replace the second letter of each word to give two new words. Write this letter in the space provided; together the replacement letters spell out a famous name.

ACES	_____	AJAR
BIDE	_____	BUCK
ORYX	_____	ACTS
EMIT	_____	ISLE
SPUN	_____	CLIP
PACK	_____	LUCK

Answers on page 187   Score **1 point** for each correct answer   **Your score** _____

27 CAESAR CIPHER

Decryption of codes is a specific application of logical aptitude. One of the simplest forms of code writing is letter substitution, where one letter is replaced with another. The simple cipher supposedly employed by Julius Caesar is created by simply shifting one or more letters to the right in the alphabet, so that, in a single-shift cipher for instance, A is written as B, B as C, and so on. In a triple-shift cipher, A→D, B→E, and so on. Given the specified shifts, decode the ciphertexts below and reveal their true meaning.

	Shift	**Cipher text**	**Answer**
A	**1**	**SPNBOT**	_____
B	**2**	**YJKURGT**	_____
C	**2**	**JKFFGP**	_____
D	**3**	**VHFUHW**	_____

Answers on page 187
Score **1 point** for each decryption   **Your score** _____

28 SECRET MESSAGE

Can you use a triple-shift Caesar cipher to encode this message?

URGENT MESSAGE, MEET CONTACT TONIGHT

Answer_____

Answer on page 187
Score **2 points** for encoding correctly Your score _____

29 BLACK AND WHITE

Below are the names of five black and white animals, encoded using a Caesar cipher. Can you work out the shift of the cipher from the cipher text, and identify all the animals?

RCPFC _____

BGDTC _____

UMWPM _____

DCFIGT _____

RGPIWKP _____

Shift _____

Answers on page 187
Score **1 point** for identifying each animal and **1 point** for working out the shift Your score _____

30 SPOT THE E

Here is a cipher text written in a Caesar cipher. Can you use frequency analysis of the letters (see Tip, below) to work out the letter shift of this cipher?

JQJAJS JQJUMFSYX JCNYJI YMJ JQJAFYTW JCHQFNRNSL JCHNYJIQD

Answer _____

Answer on page 187   Score **2 points** for a correct answer Your score _____

> **TIP**
>
> When trying to break a code, you can look for certain clues. For example, in most languages some letters are much more common than others: in English the most common letter is E; 12.7% of letters in a typical English text are the letter E. The next most common letter in English is T, with a frequency of 9.1%. Breaking a code by counting the letters is known as "frequency analysis."

31 MORSE CODE

Morse code was invented to allow transmission of letters and numbers by simple pulses of sound/electricity. Using the chart on the right, can you translate the following words into Morse code?

A MIND _____

B TRAIN _____

C SPEAR _____

D BUFFALO _____

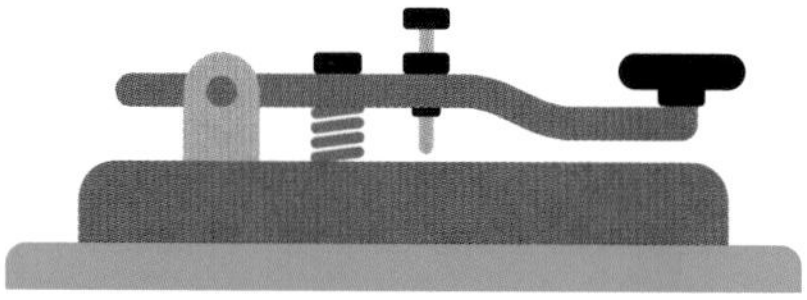

A	B	C	D	E	F	G
.-	-...	-.-.	-..	.	..-.	--.
H	**I**	**J**	**K**	**L**	**M**	**N**
....	..	.---	-.-	.-..	--	-.
O	**P**	**Q**	**R**	**S**	**T**	**U**
---	.--.	--.-	.-.	...	-	..-
V	**W**	**X**	**Y**	**Z**		
...-	.--	-..-	-.--	--..		

Answers on page 187   Score **1 point** for 4/4   Your score _____

32 EMERGENCY TRANSMISSION

You are operating the wireless on a ship sailing across the Pacific when you pick up this message. Using the chart in exercise 31, can you decode it? (Forward slashes indicate the break between words.)

... --- ... / ... .--. .-- .-. . -.-. -.- . .-.. / --- -. / -.-. --- .-.. .- .-.. / .. ... .-.. .- -. -.

Answer _____

Answer on page 187   Score **2 points** for a correct answer   Your score _____

33 RIVERBOAT CROSSING

You have to transport a fox, a chicken, and a bag of corn across a river. On each trip across the river, your boat can only carry you and one of the others, but the problem is that if you leave the fox with the chicken, or the chicken with the corn, one of them will get eaten. How do you get all three to the other side of the river?

Answer _____

_____

_____

Answer on page 187
Score 3 points for getting everything safely across the river Your score _____

34 INTO THE DESERT

You need to deliver a message from Fort Beau to Fort Geste, which takes six days of travel across arid, scorching desert. You have three camels and two other legionnaires to help you, but each camel can only carry enough water to last itself and a rider for four days. What is the minimum number of camels you need to deliver the message safely to Fort Geste without leaving yourself or any other legionnaires stranded in the desert?

Answer _____

_____

_____

Answer on page 187
Score 3 points for a correct answer Your score _____

Your score   **/65**   **60+ GOLD**

You are able to approach problems logically, focusing clearly on what the questions are asking and thinking through your answers. See the Challenge for ways to be logical in daily life.

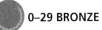 **30–59 SILVER**

You are succeeding up to a point, but possibly the harder questions are tripping you up. Try the Challenge on page 179 for tips on how to practice logical thinking.

 0–29 BRONZE

Your logic reasoning needs work. Possibly you rushed to give your answers without properly thinking through them, or let yourself be overwhelmed by the problems. Try them again using methodical reasoning.

★ Turn to page 179 for the Challenge

CHAPTER 13
SPARK OF GENIUS
CREATIVITY

Spark of genius

Pinning down the definition and mechanism of creativity is difficult, but research has shown ways in which creativity can be stimulated and lubricated. This chapter introduces a variety of exercises designed to stimulate and/or unblock the creative powers you already possess, as well as looking at how to boost them further.

QUESTIONNAIRE

Is your mind alive with vistas of visionary splendor or do you daydream about spreadsheets? Answer the questions in this quick quiz to find out just how creative you are.

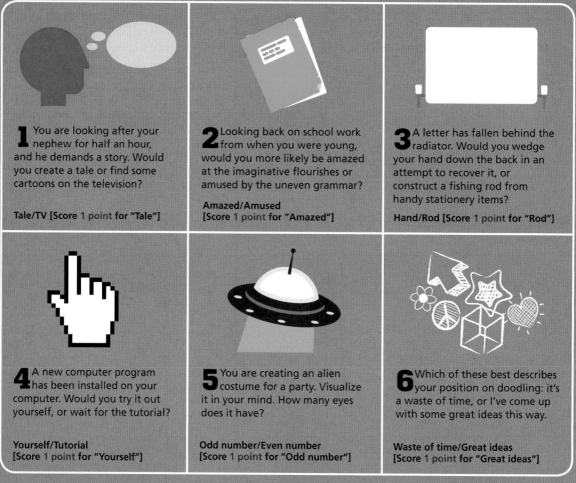

1 You are looking after your nephew for half an hour, and he demands a story. Would you create a tale or find some cartoons on the television?

Tale/TV [Score **1** point for **"Tale"**]

2 Looking back on school work from when you were young, would you more likely be amazed at the imaginative flourishes or amused by the uneven grammar?

Amazed/Amused
[Score **1** point for **"Amazed"**]

3 A letter has fallen behind the radiator. Would you wedge your hand down the back in an attempt to recover it, or construct a fishing rod from handy stationery items?

Hand/Rod [Score 1 point for **"Rod"**]

4 A new computer program has been installed on your computer. Would you try it out yourself, or wait for the tutorial?

Yourself/Tutorial
[Score **1** point **for "Yourself"**]

5 You are creating an alien costume for a party. Visualize it in your mind. How many eyes does it have?

Odd number/Even number
[Score **1** point for **"Odd number"**]

6 Which of these best describes your position on doodling: it's a waste of time, or I've come up with some great ideas this way.

Waste of time/Great ideas
[Score **1** point for **"Great ideas"**]

How did you score?
0–2: You think of yourself as a straightforward type. This doesn't mean you don't have the creative potential, simply that you are not used to unleashing it. The exercises in this chapter could help.

3–4: You have innate creativity, but you are probably not aware of the simple tricks you can use to boost this. Work through the exercises in this chapter to find out more.
5–6: You have a powerful imagination. See how original you can be as you work through this chapter.

1 ONE WORD FITS ALL

The ability to use the same word in different contexts or, better still, in constructions of widely divergent meaning, is a marker of creativity, and particularly of creative faculty with language. It is known as the "remote associates" test. Psychologists use this exercise to test a person's creativity. For each of the word triplets below, can you find a word that fits with all of them to make a recognized phrase or word? For example, if you had the words "sleep," "way," and "moon," the answer would be "walk."

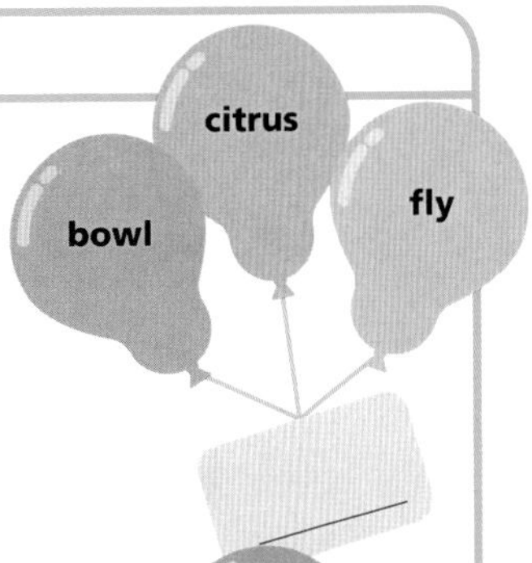

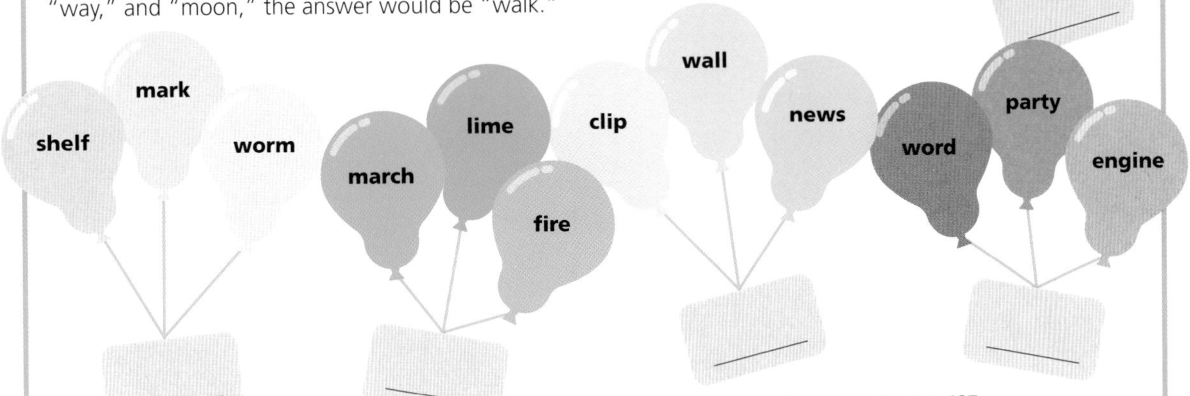

citrus

bowl

fly

mark

wall

party

shelf

worm

lime

clip

news

word

engine

march

fire

Answers on page 187

2 CREATIVE CATEGORIZATION

Creativity is sometimes characterized as the ability to make new connections, especially connections that are not obvious or familiar. Try out this aspect of creativity by coming up with new ways to connect the objects shown below by organizing them into groups in novel and unexpected ways. How many ways of categorizing them can you come up with in five minutes? Try to make the categories as original as possible.

3 THINK OF THE OPPOSITE

A popular creativity-stimulating exercise that forces you to think in novel ways and challenge preconceptions is to conceptualize opposites. This exercise can be used for everything from marketing strategies to technological goals. Stimulate your gray matter by coming up with an opposite to the following concepts. There are no right or wrong answers, but don't mistake "absence of" for "opposite"—for instance, the opposite of gravity is not "weightlessness."

omelette _____

design _____

diary _____

wine _____

eagle _____

4 FLIP IT

Related to finding the opposite is turning on its head your "normal thinking" about something. This forces you into novel conceptualizations. On a separate piece of paper, write down the five reasons requested in each scenario below.

You inherit a sum of money from a relative. Give five reasons why this is bad news.

You are at a restaurant and your main course is delicious and served at just the right temperature. List five reasons why you would send it back.

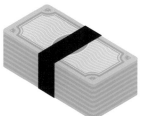

Getting out of the shower you slip and break your ankle. Give five reasons why you are lucky this happened.

You have a pile of dirty laundry to do. List five reasons why this is good news.

5 ALTERNATIVE USES

The standard test in experiments researching factors that influence creativity is called the "alternative uses" test. Your task is to come up with as many alternative uses as possible for an everyday object in a limited time. Try to be as original and imaginative as you can. Allowing two minutes for each, see how many alternative uses you can write down on a separate piece of paper for each of these objects:

paperclip   **whisk**   **newspaper**   **pencil sharpener**

6 DOODLE DESIGN

Doodling is a good way to be creative in an accessible everyday context. It's not the quality of your drawing that counts but the novelty of your design. Explore your creativity here by creating a scene on the grid, right. You must follow these two rules: you can only draw horizontal and vertical lines (no diagonals allowed), and your scene must include the colored boxes.

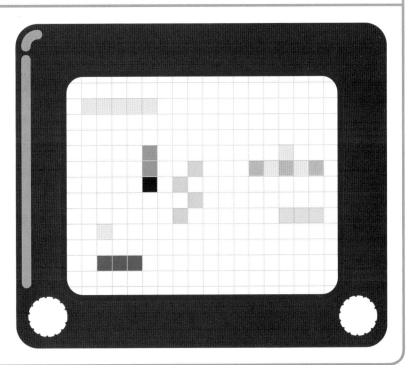

7 FANTASTIC VOYAGE

Challenge your creative flair further. A mad inventor has sent you his initial drawing for a revolutionary new vehicle (see below). Complete the blueprint and design the strangest and most original craft ever to drive, fly, float, or dive—or do all four!

8 UNDER THE SEA

Visualize a creature in the murky depths of the ocean. Now sketch it in the space below. Don't read the text at the bottom of the page until you have finished.

How many eyes, arms, tentacles, and such like does your creature have? Is it symmetrical? Research suggests that when creativity is flowing freely, the creatures that people sketch are less symmetrical and less constrained by the rules of terrestrial anatomy.

9 JAILBREAK

You are trapped at the top of a tower, with nothing for company except the array of unusual objects pictured below. On a separate piece of paper, can you come up with an escape plan that cunningly employs every one of the objects—the more far-fetched and fantastical the better.

ice cube

rope

chewing gum

hat

piano key

bird seed

crossbow

chalk

comb

mirror

10 FAIRY TALE BLITZ

Pressure to create can produce some unusual results. See this for yourself with this exercise. Below are typical elements from a fairy tale. You have 10 minutes to write down, on a separate piece of paper, the plots of three different fairy tales, each involving all of the elements depicted.

princess

frog

apple

tree

spinning wheel

fox

ogre

mirror

bean stalk

11 JEOPARDY

Can you work backward from each of the punchlines below and, on a separate piece of paper, come up with a funny story that leads up to it, using no more than five sentences?

…and that's why you never let a monkey give you a haircut!

…so the sailor says to the king, "I'm sorry, sir, we don't take American Express."

…and the last one to get his shoes back was the Ambassador.

…and the sign said, "You don't have to work here to be mad, but it helps."

TIP

Research shows that the simple technique of putting mental distance between you and a problem can help stimulate creative thinking about the problem. For instance, if you have to solve a problem about someone you work with, think about how another person far away or from a different era might solve the problem. Putting temporal or spatial distance between you and the problem can boost the creativity of your response.

12 STORY CORNERS

Writers who struggle to get their creative juices flowing sometimes do quick creative writing exercises. Here is an example—the beginning and end of a story are supplied below. On a separate piece of paper, can you write the intervening narrative? You can write as much as you want, but aim for at least 100 words.

It was a dark and steamy night. A shot rang out, and a car slipped quietly out of the warehouse and over the edge of the wharf, into the greasy waters of the Hudson…

…Jerrod put his feet up on the table and took a long drink from a short glass. It had been his toughest case yet, and except for the ruined photographs, the the missing suspect, and the stolen pistol, he thought it had all gone rather well.

13 HOLLYWOOD HOKUM

On a separate piece of paper, come up with titles and one-line synopses for the following film posters.

How did you do?

There is no scoring in this chapter, so assess yourself subjectively.

I WAS INSPIRED

If you found these exercises inspiring and enjoyable, then see if you can transfer these skills to other aspects of intelligence and use them to enhance your all-round cognitive performance. For instance, creative visualization is a powerful tool for memory-enhancing performance.

I DID OKAY

Did some of the exercises inspire you more than others? Go back and see what the common factors were for the tasks that fired your creativity. Perhaps you can use these as triggers for creativity in other scenarios.

I STRUGGLED

If you found the exercises difficult and time-consuming, consider your working environment when approaching the tasks. Try out the Challenge on page 179 to get into a more creative frame of mind.

 Turn to page 179 for the Challenge.

Challenges

How did you find the exercises throughout the book? If your score for a chapter was low, or you felt as if you struggled on a certain chapter, then try the relevant Challenge below. Even if you succeeded in the chapters, these Challenges will help boost your brain power further.

CHAPTER 1

INSTANT REVIEW
Practice instant reviewing (immediately going over new information in your head or out loud) so that it becomes a habit. Repeat phone numbers, license plates, shopping lists, people's names, and such on an everyday basis to help kickstart the transfer of information from STM to intermediate memory, where it won't fade as quickly.

CHAPTER 2

THE OTHER HALF
Set yourself the target of memorizing the names of the partners of all the people with whom you share an office or gym class or any suitable group of people you wish. Start off by writing down a list, and then use memory techniques that form associations between the people you know and their partners' names. Test yourself after a week, a month, and three months, and see if you find the names easier to recall after a period of time has passed.

CHAPTER 3

DOORSTEP ROUTINE
A good habit to get into is making a house-leaving routine, which you practice on the doorstep before you close the door. Pat your pockets or look inside your bag and run through a mental checklist. Keys? Check! Wallet? Check! Travel pass? Check!

CHAPTER 4

BANK REVIEW
A good way to give your MTM a workout is to sit down with an itemized bank statement and work through the cash payments you have made in the last few days or weeks. Cover the place details, leaving only the amounts and the dates and try to recall the relevant locations.

CHAPTER 5

DAILY REVIEW
If you're trying to improve your biographical memory, you need to improve your encoding. One tactic is to get into the habit of reviewing your activities and experiences at the end of each day. Without question the best way to do this is to keep a journal, but even if you just take 5 minutes to run through things in your head it should help.

CHAPTER 6

NOW YOU SEE IT
Create visualizations for each of your PINs to make them easier to recall. For example, you could link the shape of each number to an object: the number 1 could remind you of a pencil, for example, and the number 4 might make a sailboat spring to mind. Once you have your objects relating to the numbers, combine them to make one memorable image and practice recalling the image when you need to remember your PIN. You can also incorporate into your visualization the color of the card the PIN goes with to further boost recollection of which PIN relates to which card.

CHAPTER 7

SYSTEM ADDICT

A systematic approach to revision can boost the efficiency and efficacy of learning. Use a 5-stage system. 1. Preview the material by skimming to get an idea of its content. 2. Make a list of questions to answer when you're finished. 3. Read through the material with the goal of finding answers to your questions. 4. Summarize what you've learned by reviewing the main points. 5. Test yourself within 24 hours by writing answers to the questions you asked earlier.

CHAPTER 8

CHANGE FOR THE BETTER

Use mental arithmetic whenever paying for something with cash. Get into the habit of mentally adding up the cost of the goods you are buying. Work out in your head the change that will be due when you pay before the cashier does the calculation for you.

CHAPTER 9

GRAPH YOUR LIFE

Turn real-world scenarios into graphs. Any situation in which one variable changes according to another, and numbers are involved, can be graphed. For instance, you could draw a graph of how your salary has changed over time, or how your weight has changed with age. Not only is this good exercise for your numerical intelligence, but it can also give you an interesting new angle on things.

CHAPTER 10

LEVEL UP YOUR READING

Improve your vocabulary and all-round verbal aptitude by reading more books, journals, and newspapers. Keep a notepad and pencil handy and get into the habit of writing down words you don't know and looking them up later. Make a point of trying to use each new word you have learned in conversation on a regular basis.

CHAPTER 11

ANTIPODEAN MOUSE

A simple exercise to get your visuo-spatial processes working (specifically, the activity in the cerebellum, the area at the back of the brain that controls coordination) is to turn your computer mouse 180 degrees and try creating a picture in a drawing program with it.

CHAPTER 12

LOGIC

Cryptography is a form of logical reasoning—start an encrypted correspondence with someone, and challenge each other to break codes of your own devising.

CHAPTER 13

MEDITATION FOR CREATIVITY

State of mind is believed to be an important influence on creativity and your ability to think creatively. Anxiety and distractions tend to sap creativity, but a clear, focused mind can dramatically enhance it. Set aside 5 minutes every day to sit quietly and observe what is happening around you. Then see if you can create a short story linking events you can see, as your creative thoughts start to surface.

Solutions

CHAPTER 1

2 WHERE DID YOU GET THAT HAT?

The baseball cap is the odd one out because it is the only hat with a peak.

6 CAN YOU CUT IT?

10 DRAWING WITH YOUR MIND'S EYE

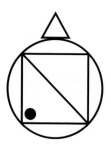

11 DUCKS IN A ROW

14 TREASURE ISLAND

You end up at the red hut.

24 INTERFERING OBJECTS

The escalator is the odd one out because it's the only one that moves you. All the others you have to work manually.

25 INTERFERING NUMBERS

The jack of clubs.

CHAPTER 3

16 LEFT AND RIGHT

You end up at the church.

CHAPTER 6

2 LEETSPEAK

A GOBULLDOGS = 9*|3|_|11|)*9$
B XYLOPHONE = %'/,1*IO#*|\3
C BIRTHDAY = |3!|27#|)@'/,
D CALORIES = (@1*|2!3$
E WHITEHOUSE = VV#!73#*|_|$3

3 STACKED UP

A 4046 = rfvp;/rfvyhn
B 1979 = qazol.ujmol.
C 2005 = wsxp;/p;/tgb
D 8238 = ik,wsxedcik,

4 BASE SYSTEM

A A41A14A
B IA16GO17
C 3BMSHTR
D ATWI80D

5 SYSTEM ADDICT
A 5TULOB
B 7YCAGWYW
C 4TKAM
D 6RSANSD

6 BESPOKE PASSWORDS
A gre10TTBBITFOTN
B eve10TTBBITFOTN
C y3k10TTBBITFOTN
D leg10TTBBITFOTN

7 CONSONANT SWAP
A 10TTEEITFOTN
B 10ETEBITUATN
C 10TTBBOUFOTN
D 10TEBAITEOTN

8 MADE TO MEASURE
A gree10TT
B even10TT
C y3ks10TT
D lega10TT

11 UP STACKED
A 5354
B 8902
C 6232
D 9715

15 LETTER PAIRS PLUS
A ASPP = 0855
B TCJT = 9299
C WABO = 2014
D EPMG = 4526

18 THIS OLD MAN
A 2187
B 0645
C 2934

CHAPTER 7

1 QUIZ MASTER
1 India
2 Beethoven
3 Atlantic, Arctic, Indian, Pacific, Southern
4 "For every action there is an equal and opposite reaction."
5 China
6 1917
7 Buzz Aldrin
8 Femur (thighbone)
9 Uruguay
10 Walt Disney. He won 26 oscars

2 SPOT THE LINK
They are all landlocked countries (they have no coastline).

CHAPTER 8

1 ARITHMETIC 101
A 1,221
B 13,203
C 246
D 3,274
E 693
F 6,612
G 11
H 13

2 RAISING CHANGE
A $4.15
B $1.05
C $8.95
D $1.02

3 PAPERBACK PROBLEM
The Secret Life of Aunts and Year of the Yak ($16.98). Your change will be $0.52.

4 CANDY CONUNDRUM
Answer: 21

5 ARE YOU COORDINATED?
A -2, -3
B 2, 9
C 7, 5
D 4, 1
E 6, -4

6 COINS
There are 600 coins in the wooden chest and 1,400 in the steel chest

7 WHICH IS BIGGER? EASY
1 $7/8$
2 $3/4$
3 $2/3$
4 $9/16$
5 $2/5$
6 $5/15$

8 WHICH IS BIGGER? TOUGH
1 $9/12$
2 $2/3$
3 $5/8$
4 $6/10$
5 $8/15$
6 $15/32$

9 DECIMALS VS FRACTIONS I
1 0.8
2 $2/3$
3 0.6
4 $2/6$
5 0.3
6 $1/4$

10 DECIMALS VS FRACTIONS II
1 $11/21$
2 0.5
3 $2/5$
4 0.333
5 0.275
6 $7/32$

continued →

CHAPTER 8 continued

11 SOCK PUZZLE
Answer: 20

12 SLICE OF THE PIE
A
1 ½
2 ¼
3 ¼
B
1 ¼
2 ⅙
3 ⅙
4 ⅙
5 ¼
C
1 ⅓
2 ⅑
3 ⅑
4 ⅑
5 ⅓
D
1 ¼
2 ⅛
3 ⅛
4 ¼
5 ⅛
6 ⅛

13 STAR STRUCK
Answer: 75% ¾ of 160 = 120; 90/120 = ¾ (75%)

14 LITTLE BROTHER
Answer: 6

15 CHEESE PLEASE
A $13.41
B $14.10
C $19.52

16 HENRY'S CAT
Answer: 16

17 BILL TEASER
A 10
B 5
C 5
D 5

18 WHAT TIME IS IT? I
A 9am
B 1am
C 8pm
D 13 hours; 6pm

19 WHAT TIME IS IT? II
A 10:59am
B 10:17am
C 5:18pm and 5:48pm
D City Cinema

20 MISSING NUMBER
Answer: 9. The final square in each row is the sum of the first two squares.

21 CURRENCY COVERTER
A $800
B £200
C £12.50
D €250
E 25,000 Yen

22 WEIGHTS AND MEASURES
A 14/2.2 = 6.36kg
B 100/2.54 = 39.37in
C 1.0936 x 3 or 39.37/12 = 3.28ft
D 1/1.0936 = 0.9144m
E 3.28 x 0.9144 = 3ft
F 1,000/28.35 = 35.27oz
G 35.27/2.2 = 16oz
H 16 x 14 = 224oz

23 BARGAIN BIKE HUNTER
The second shop. The original price in the first shop is $400, and $350 in the second shop.

24 DJ BATTLE
Track 13. Wilfred's playlist is 4, 7, 10, 13, so Miles' must be 13, 9, 5, 1.

CHAPTER 9

1 CALCULATOR CRISIS
A –
B ÷
C +
D x

2 PRIME TIME
Answer: 13, 17, 19, 23, 29, 31, 37, 41, 43, 47

3 SHARED SECRET
They are all products of prime numbers (5x5 = 25; 3x17 = 51; 7x17 = 119)

4 AVERAGE APPLES
Answer: 4.2oz. The average is the combined weight of all the apples divided by the total number of apples. The combined weight is found by multiplying the weight categories by the number in each category: (67x3.9) + (32x3.4) + (125x4.6) + (16x4.0) = 261.3+108.8+575+64 = 1,009; total number apples = 240; 1,009/240 = 4.2oz

5 NUMBER TRIANGLE I
Answer: 16. The numbers in the center are the sum of the bottom right number and the product of the other two numbers: 65 – (7x7) = 16

6 NUMBER TRIANGLE II
Answer: 4. The central number is found by dividing the product of the top number and the bottom left number by the bottom right number: (8x3)÷6 = 4

7 NUMBER CROSS I

Answer: 13. The middle number is the sum of the individual digits of the top and bottom number and also the left and right number: 4+2+1+6 = 13; 5+0+3+5 = 13

8 NUMBER CROSS II

Answer: 10. The middle number is the difference between the difference between the top and bottom numbers and the difference between the left and right numbers: (42–26) – (31–25) = 16–6 = 10

9 NUMBER PENTAGON

In each pentagon, starting from the top right number and top numbers and finishing with the central number, the numbers are the sums of the previous two numbers.

A 21(13+8 = 21)

B 22 (34–12 = 22)

C 9 and 25 (66–41= 25; 25–16 = 9)

D 4, 8, and 20 (32–12 = 20, 20–12 = 8, 8–4 = 4)

10 NUMBER SQUARE

Answer: 42. In each row, the last column is the product of the third column and the difference between the first two columns: (8–2) x 7 = 42

11 WHERE ANGLES FEAR TO TREAD

A 60°

B 50°

C 30°

D 1 = 55°; 2 = 90°

E 1 = 27°; 3 = 90°

12 IN THE AREA

A 24

B 9

C 4

D 4

E area = 28.26; circumference = 18.84

F area = 50.24; circumference = 25.12

13 FLOOR SPACE

Answer: 527sq ft

14 ALGEBRA ALERT

A 0.60

B 6

C 3

D 5

E 4

15: GRAPH IT

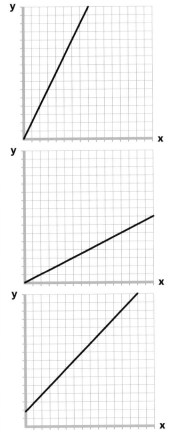

16 LEARNING CURVE

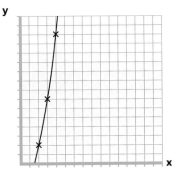

CHAPTER 10

1 FROM A TO Z

1 apple

2 bottle

3 crown

4 headphones

5 ladder

6 mouse

7 tree

8 wristwatch

9 xylophone

10 zipper

2 FROM S TO S

1 sedan

2 sedation

3 sedative

4 sedentary

5 sedimentary

6 sedimentation

7 seditious

8 seduction

9 seductive

10 sedulous

3 FILL IN THE GAPS

The scarecrow **guarded** the field **but** the crows **ignored** the scarecrow, **squawking** at his old hat, **until** the farmer **arrived** on his tractor and **shook** his rake.

continued ➔

CHAPTER 10 continued

4 SYNONYMS

A Technical and artful

B Graceful and lithe

C Eerie and macabre

D Nimble and spry

5 SYNONYMS BY ANALOGY

A Mendacity

B Fragile

C Semaphore

D Virtuous

6 ANTONYMS

A Sustain and deny

B Puerile and mature

C Expedite and hinder

D Colorful and drab

7 ANTONYMS BY ANALOGY

A Radiancy

B Unrestrained

C Loosen

D Diffident

8 LETTER COUNTING

There are many answers for each amount. Here is an example for each.

A TUMBLER

B JEOPARDY

C EXAMS

D HOB

9 WORD GRID

PREVENTATIVE

10 ODD ONE OUT

A PLAINFAST. The others can be made into words by swapping round the syllables.

B YRINGE. The others can be made into a word by replacing the first letter with the letter S.

12 UPSIDE DOWN READING

A A fortress to protect Paris from Viking attacks.

B François I.

C I. M. Pei.

15 FRUIT SALAD

A Banana

B Grapefruit

C Cauliflower

D Watermelon

E Black currant

F Pineapple

G Clementine

Cauliflower (C) is the odd one out because it is the only vegetable.

16 ANAGRAM DETECTIVE

A Sleuth

B Monarchy

C Notebook

D Religion

E Umpire

F Invention

CHAPTER 11

1 SPOT THE DIFFERENCE

2 FLOOR PLANNER

Answer: 505sq ft

3 GET YOUR HEAD AROUND THIS

Answer: D. The others are all rotations. D is a mirror image of C.

4 AMBASSADORIAL AMBUSH

Answer: B. The red squares have been flipped.

5 TOUGH ROTATION

Answer: E. The others all have identical pairs in different rotations: A and G; B and D; C and F.

6 ABOUT FACE

Answer: C

7 A CUBE WITH A VIEW
Answer: A

8 UNPACKING
Answer: D. All the others could be views of the same cube—only in view A does the arrangement of sides not match up with what is shown in the other views.

9 WHERE IN THE WORLD?

10 MAP MAKER

11 REFRIGERATOR PACKER

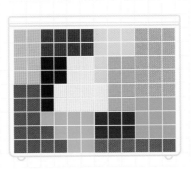

12 TILE GAME
Answer: B

13 CHESS MOVES
Answer: 5

14 SHAPE SERIES I
Answer: B

15 SHAPE SERIES II
Answer: A

16 STRIKE A POSE
Answer: B. The left arm moves down and the right leg moves up by 45°. The right arm then moves down and the left leg up by 45°.

17 TELLTALE SHAPES I
Answer: C. The purple shapes have a vertical line of symmetry.

18 TELLTALE SHAPES II
Answer: B. The blue circle is moving along the diagonal, one square at a time; the black circle is shifting left to right; and the triangle is shifting right to left.

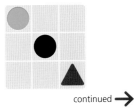

continued →

CHAPTER 11 continued

19 ALPHABET STREET
Answer: R

CHAPTER 12

1 WHICH ANIMAL IS NEXT?
Skunk (the sequence is stripes, spots, stripes, spots, so the next animal must be striped).

2 MATERIAL WORLD
Diamond (the sequence goes from least valuable by weight to most valuable).

3 THE DAY TODAY
Answer: Friday

4 ALPHABET DIRECTIONS
Answer: I

5 REASONING BY ANALOGY
Answer: D. 6 is 2/3 of 9, so 2/3 of 12 is 8 (D).

6 PEACEMAKER
C: LIVE. The numbers correspond to their position in the alphabet (P=16/26; E=5/26; etc).

7 COFFEE TIME
B: 51216161. The numbers correspond to their position in the alphabet, but the answer is backward (E=5, L=12, P=16, P=16, 1=A).

8 LAW AND ORDER
Thief, crime, arrest, court, prison, parole (the logical order of events from first to last).

9 ANIMAL PLANET
Beaver, rodent, herbivore, mammal, vertebrate, animal (the classification order).

10 AIR AND SEA
Submarine, dinghy, hydrofoil, kite, blimp, jet (the order of altitude reached from lowest to highest).

11 MUSICIANS' UNION
Answer: A

12 SPORTS CLUB

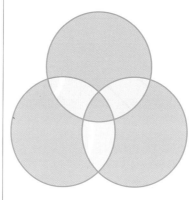

13 INTERVIEW CHOICE
Answer: 3

14 DAMAGED GOODS
Answer: 2

15 PIRATE SHIP
Answer: 17

16 TRUE OR FALSE? I
True. This isn't a trick question!

17 TRUE OR FALSE? II
False. Bill may be tall, but I may be taller. This fallacy is known as "affirming the consequent": if A, then B is not the same as B, therefore A.

18 TRUE OR FALSE? III
False. Just because A therefore C and B therefore C, doesn't mean that A therefore B is correct.

19 WHICH IS NEXT?
REGULAR (each word begins with the penultimate letter of the previous word).

20 LETTER LOGIC I
DEFIJK. The others skip one letter, this skips two.

21 LETTER LOGIC II
QDVHO. The others are all on the same line on a computer keyboard.

22 OLYMPIC CONFUSION
Gold: Armitage; Silver: Beaker; Bronze: Owembe

23 WHICH CARD?
E and 9. Most people try to confirm the hypothesis and choose E and 6. However, the hypothesis doesn't say that an even-numbered card must have a vowel on the other side.

24 SOCK SELECTOR
Answer: 3. If I pull out three socks, at least two of them must be the same color. Many people mistakenly say 21.

25 FESTIVE FOUL UP

You only need to open the "mixed" box. All the boxes are incorrectly labeled, so the "mixed" box must either be liquers or toffee. If it contains liquers, you know the box labeled "liquers" must contain toffee centers, or else one of the boxes would have the correct label, which we know is not the case.

26 LETTER CHANGER

ACES	[G]	AJAR
BIDE	[A]	BUCK
ORYX	[N]	ACTS
EMIT	[D]	ISLE
SPUN	[H]	CLIP
PACK	[I]	LUCK

27 CAESAR CIPHER

A ROMANS
B WHISPER
C HIDDEN
D SECRET

28 SECRET MESSAGE

XUJHQW PHVVDJH PHHW FRQWDFW WRQLJKW

29 CRACK THE CODE

RCPFC [PANDA]
BGDTC [ZEBRA]
UMWPM [SKUNK]
DCFIGT [BADGER]
RGPIWKP [PENGUIN]
This is a double shift cipher.

30 SPOT THE E

5-letter shift. The plain text is ELEVEN ELEPHANTS EXITED THE ELEVATOR EXCLAIMING EXCITEDLY

31 MORSE CODE

A -- .. -. -..
B - .-. .- .. -.
C ... .--. . -. .-.
D -... ..- ..-. ..-. .- .-.. ---

32 EMERGENCY TRANSMISSION

SOS SHIPWRECKED ON CORAL ISLAND

33 RIVER BOAT CROSSING

Carry the chicken across first, leave it on the far bank, come back for the corn, drop off the corn and pick up the chicken and take it back to the left bank, swap it for the fox, drop off the fox and come back for the chicken.

34 INTO THE DESERT

All three camels set off, but after one day's travel the first camel transfers a day's water to each of the other camels, keeping only the single day's water needed to get back to Fort Beau. After another day's travel, the second camel transfers one day's water to your camel, keeping two days' water to get back to Fort Beau. Meanwhile your camel still has four days' water left, enabling you to reach Fort Geste and deliver the vital message.

CHAPTER 13

1 ONE WORD FITS ALL

A Book
B Quick
C Paper
D Fruit
E Search

Useful websites

GENERAL INFORMATION ON MEMORY

www.dana.org

www.gloo.com.au

www.memorise.org

www.memory-loss.org

www.newscientist.com/topic/brain
For more information and the latest research into how the brain works

www.pbs.org/wnet/brain/

www.sharpbrains.com

www.youramazingbrain.org/yourmemory/

MEMORY TECHNIQUES

www.buildyourmemory.com

www.buzanworld.com

www.changingminds.org/techniques/memory/peg

www.mindtools.com

www.worldmemorychampionships.com

www.youramazingbrain.org/yourmemory

MORE PUZZLES

Creativity

www.cul.co.uk/creative/puzzles.htm

www.learning-tree.org.uk

Long-term memory

www.lumosity.com

www.memoryjoggingpuzzles.com

Memory and creativity

www.cul.co.uk/creative/puzzles.htm

www.enchantedmind.com/html/science/creative_memory.html

www.supplementsformemorytips.com/Improve-Memory-When-You-Improve-Creativity.html

Memory and organization

www.npmanagement.org/Article_List/Articles/Organizational_Memory.htm

www.web-us.com/memory/improving_memory.htm

Numerical reasoning

www.cut-the-knot.com

www.jimloy.com
For numerical riddles

www.krazydad.com
For Kakuro puzzles

www.riddles.com
For creative conundrums

www.visualmathlearning.com

Remembering names and faces

www.howtoimprovememory.org/names-faces/

www.memory-key.com/improving/strategies/everyday/remembering-names-faces

www.mymemoryfix.com/remember_faces.html

Remembering numbers

www.braingle.com/mind/test_numbers.php

www.memorise.org/lesson3.htm

Short-term memory

www.everydayhealth.com/longevity/mental-fitness/brain-exercises-for-memory.aspx

www.free-sudoku-puzzles.com/games/memory-game/short-term-memory-game.php

www.fupa.com/play/Puzzles-free-games/short-term-memory

www.onlinegamescastle.com/game/short-term-memory

www2.stetson.edu/~efriedma/puzzle
For a huge range of puzzles

Verbal reasoning

www.puzzlechoice.com
For crosswords, word searches, and word play games

www.wordplays.com
For more verbal games

Visual reasoning and spatial awareness

www.mycoted.com

www.sharpbrains.com

Index

About the author

Joel Levy is a science writer and journalist with a special interest in psychology. His writing explores both mainstream and fringe psychology, from cognitive boosting to anomalous experiences.After taking degrees in molecular biology and psychology at Warwick and Edinburgh universities, he has gone on to write books including *Boost Your IQ* and *Train Your Brain*.

About the illustrator

Keith Hagan's richly varied career in the graphic arts spans the disciplines of illustration, film special effects animation, graphic design and art direction, and commercial copywriting. He continues to create visual and written material for publishing, advertising, and corporate clients.

Author's acknowledgments

Thanks to Lizzie Yeates and the rest of the team behind the book: Angela Baynham, Miranda Harvey, Harriet Yeomans and Keith Hagan. Special thanks also to Dawn Henderson. Personal dedication to Anne Hooper, an inspiration and a heroic source of support.

Publisher's acknowledgments

DK Publishing would like to thank Michele Clarke for supplying the index and Claire Cross for proofreading. Many thanks also to Nikki Sims for checking the puzzles and exercises, and to Roger Trevena and Jill Hamilton for checking the puzzles in the two mathematical chapters.